Illustrated

GAMES, RHYTHMS, and STUNTS

for CHILDREN

FRANK H. GERI
DIRECTOR OF PLAYGROUNDS
BELLINGHAM, WASHINGTON

UPPER ELEMENTARY GRADES

ENGLEWOOD CLIFFS, N.J. 1957 PRENTICE-HALL, INC.

PRINTED IN THE UNITED STATES OF AMERICA

45105

"**What can we do now?**" In answer to that age-old childhood question, intelligent leadership and wise selection of recreation activities determine whether fun is to be destructive or developmental.

Whether Mother is providing entertainment for an afternoon, or the elementary school teacher is administering a broad and varied program in personality improvement through recreation, each is conducting a learning experience that can be profitable and impressive to the child. But the activities must have purpose, plan, and significance. This book makes such activities available for children between the ages of nine and twelve.

Soccer, basketball, and **softball** sections have simple drills in passing, catching, dribbling, shooting, or throwing—whichever are appropriate to the sport being taught. Lead-up games, low-organized games, and relays add to the interest and further proficiency.

The child must learn each movement by itself and practice until performance becomes natural and easy. Logically, teaching the skills would be the first step in presenting any sport, but it is often found that boys and girls of the upper elementary age are not interested in the skill and drill but in the *game*. The sport should therefore be introduced by a lead-up game. As the child becomes aware of his awkwardness and realizes that his inability to play a good game is the result of a lack of skill, he will work to perfect his playing ability, and skill will have meaning. The child will develop better playing skills while under the direction of a leader and will then take the ideas and theory home and be interested in spending many hours practicing and perfecting the skill by himself in the backyard, a spare room, or a nearby play area.

Never should a child be expected to reach a standard beyond his ability, but he should be encouraged to do his best. The program in the book is arranged in a progressive sequence, so that the needs of the children are met and their interests are satisfied.

In the early years, the child's growth in coordination is developed through an active program of low-organized games. Each of these games involves a small part of the necessary skill of the team sport. An example of this is **Line Soccer,** which develops the player's ability in kicking, blocking, and trapping as it is used in soccer.

In a lead-up game, the skills involved should be practiced and executed as they will be used in the game to follow. Learning in the lead-up games carries over into the team sport. An excellent example of this is the difficulty that arises in teaching boys and girls not to run with a basketball in their hands after they have once been allowed to do so.

The sports program should be based upon the interests of the children, and games should be taught during the season when the child's interest is at a peak. The similarity between soccer and football skills makes soccer an appropriate game for autumn. Basketball in basketball season, and softball in baseball season constitute a good schedule for presenting the games.

The success of any instructional program in sports is dependent upon the planning and presentation of the activity. The enthusiasm of the teacher, father, neighborhood leader, or coach produces a psychological reaction and will have a decided effect on the outcome of the skill or game.

The illustrations and descriptions of the skills and drills which are given in this book will help a leader or parent demonstrate the correct techniques. Demonstrations give the children the desire to imitate and show the pattern much more graphically than a verbal description.

The games in the **circle, tag,** and **goal game** sections have been selected carefully to give a variety of games from which to choose. Many play areas are suggested for these games, but leaders should not forget the driveway, car-port, backyard, basement, spare room, community halls, neighborhood parks, and playgrounds.

The book gives a variety of games suitable for both large and small groups. Many types of games have been included, such as: running, quiet, pair, hide-seek, keep-away, capture, object exchange, dramatic, skill, and "It" games. Games have been planned for group or pack meetings, picnics and parties, sidewalk, and limited areas.

Adults often allow themselves too little time to enjoy the beauties and secrets of the world about them. Children love to hike and camp out, and parents and leaders can enjoy and learn with their children about plants, trees, birds, fish, stars, and animals. Games in the nature section are both fun and educational.

From times of old, children have played **Hop Scotch, Jacks,** or **Roly Poly** on the sidewalk, but directions are not always easily secured, for the games found in the sidewalk section are like legends or sagas. They are often handed down from parents or older brothers and sisters. The author has recognized this problem and has included many rules and variations that may stimulate the imaginations of children and their leaders. Parents will enjoy playing many of these games with the children, and the children will be more than pleased to have the parents play with them.

Rhythms are an essential part of every boy's and girl's social, physical, and emotional growth and should be included in many programs for the nine-, ten-, eleven-, and twelve-year-olds. Parents and leaders play a definite role in determining the interest of the boy or girl in dancing.

It is at this stage, the upper elementary, that boys tend to separate and form their own interests. They are interested in dancing but are beginning to look to their peers for approval and recognition. If a contemporary says, "That's sissy," the boy is no longer the eager partner; thus, the leaders' role is to set the example. Class, home or club parties can include dancing. Family interest can be developed by the child's teaching the parent a dance learned in school and the parents' teaching the child a step or dance they enjoyed at a recent social gathering.

The dances offered in this book are excellent for small or large groups. In many places about the country, adults are enjoying them in their clubs, and youngsters will enjoy them also. Couple dances can be enjoyed by the family, Mother dancing with her son and Dad with his daughter.

At neighborhood get-togethers in the club house, the home, an empty garage, or barn, dances such as **The Ace of Diamonds, Captain Jinks,** and the square dances offered in the rhythm section of this book are splendid activities for the children.

Leaders of Cub Scouts, Scouts, church groups, campfire groups, 4-H and boys' and girls' clubs will find that not only is group dancing stimulating and exciting for the children, but also it is an easy way to entertain groups. Once the directions are given and the dance learned, everyone is doing the same thing at the same time, and the dances are using the tremendous amount of exuberant energy that most children have to release.

Read carefully the techniques for teaching dances. Much grief will be avoided if a careful plan of procedure is worked out before presenting the dance. Dancing is fun, but much of the fun is destroyed if the dances are introduced by someone who must work out the steps as he presents the dance.

The chapter on safety is an effort on the part of the author to prevent accidents before they happen. Necessary precautions should be taught, and children should develop the habit of thinking in terms of safety for the indivdual and the participating group. Illustrations are included to encourage safety-mindedness.

Younger and older children should be separated in play areas, particularly on a playground or at a picnic. And leaders must always observe the hazards of the surrounding area: old buildings and apparatus that tempt climbers or bordering streets from which balls must be retrieved.

The surest way of safeguarding children at play is to begin early in developing awareness of hazards and having a continuous safety program in every plan. Providing safe places for the children to play is a fundamental, but children must learn that precautions are necessary on the safest of playgrounds.

Trained leaders of physical education and recreation represent a small portion of the people who are called upon to teach and guide games and rhythms. But the untrained, the busy, and even the bewildered have as great a responsibility cast upon them as the professional. To the trained and the untrained we offer help and ideas.

FRANK H. GERI

CONTENTS

Characteristics of Intermediate Age Group 11
Suggestions 13
Preparation and Planning .. 13
Leader's Evaluation of Activity Period 14
Formations 15

TAG GAMES 17

Ante I Over 17
Ball Tag 18
Base Exchange 19
Base Tag 20
Beanbag Hop Tag 20
Catch the Pheasant 21
Chain Tag 22
Exchange 23
Hook On 24
Last Couple Out 24
Light Night 25
Mystery Tag 26
Safety Tag 27
Shoulder Tag 28
Snatch the Handkerchief .. 29
Sock 'Em Base Tag 30
Spot Tag 31
Square Tag 32
Statue Tag 33
Zoo Tag 34

CIRCLE GAMES 35

Beat the Count 35
Bird, Beast, or Fish 36
Circle Exchange Tag 37
Circle Keep Away 38
Circle Race 38
Circle Stride Ball 39

Circle Tantalizers 39
Circle Target 40
End Dodge Ball 41
General and His Men 42
Jungle Chief 43
Lame Fox and Chickens 43
Man in the Circle 44
Number Please 45
Skip around the Circle 46
Snap the Trap 47
Stormy Ocean 48

NATURE GAMES 49

Bird Description 50
Deer Stalking 51
Duplicate 52
Getting Your Partners 53
I Spy 54
Leaf Relay 54
Matching Leaves 55
Nature Alphabet 56
Nature Spy 56
Peep Hole 57
Pine Ball 58
Scavenger Hunt 59
Trailing 60

LIMITED AREA GAMES .. 61

Bell Rings 61
Bird, Flower, or Tree 62
Birds Fly 63
Fruit or Vegetable Basket .. 64
I Am a Farmer and I Know My Stock 65
Mimic the Leader 66
Object Exchange 67
Ring on the String 68

RELAYS 69	Limited Area Relays 92
Teaching Technique Hints .. 70	BEANBAG BULL'S-EYE 92
Relay Formations 71	FREIGHT TRAIN 93
Team Relays 72	KICK THE BEANBAG 94
	RING PASS RELAY 94
BOUNCE RELAY 72	RING THE BELL RELAY 96
DRIBBLE RELAY 72	SCHOOLROOM RELAY 97
ELEPHANT WALK RELAY 73	WOODEN LEG RELAY 97
INDIAN CLUB RELAY 74	
LEAPFROG RELAY 74	ROPE SKIPPING 99
OBSTACLE RELAY 76	General Information 99
ONE-HAND RELAY 76	Individual Rope Jumping ... 100
OVERHEAD PASS RELAY 77	Long Rope Doubles 102
PASS AND ZIGZAG RELAY 78	
PRONE CIRCLE RELAY 78	RHYTHMS 103
RAIL BALANCE RELAY 79	Rhythmical Objectives 103
RAINY WASH-DAY RELAY 80	Techniques for Rhythms 104
RUN AND TOSS RELAY 81	Folk and Square Dance Ter-
SPOKE-CIRCLE AND	minology 106
CLUB-SNATCH RELAY 81	Social Dance Positions 112
Pair Relays 82	Dances 113
BEANBAG HOBBLE-KICK RELAY 82	
DOUBLE HOBBLE RELAY 83	ACE OF DIAMONDS 113
ELBOW PAIR RELAY 84	BADGER GAVOTTE 114
FORWARD AND	BLEKING 115
BACKWARD RELAY 84	BLEKING STEP 116
THREE-LEGGED RELAY 85	CAPTAIN JINKS 117
	COTTON-EYED JOE 118
Shuttle Relays 85	CRESTED HEN 119
BOARD BALANCE	CSEBOGAR 120
FRONT AND BACK WALK 85	DOWN SOUTH MIXER 121
BOTTLE AND	DOWN THE CENTER AND
STICK SHUTTLE RELAY 86	DIVIDE THE RING 122
FARMER AND	GLOW WORM MIXER 124
CROW SHUTTLE RELAY 86	GUSTAF'S SKOAL 125
FORWARD-BACKWARD	HANSEL AND GRETEL 126
ROLL SHUTTLE RELAY 87	HEEL AND TOE POLKA 127
FROG AND CRAB	IRISH WASHERWOMAN MIXER 128
SHUTTLE RELAY 88	KLAPPDANS 130
KANGAROO-HOP AND GOAT-	LA RASPA 131
BUTTING SHUTTLE RELAY ... 89	LILLI MARLENE 132
LOAD DOWN SHUTTLE RELAY .. 89	LITTLE MAN IN A FIX 134
ROPE SKIP VARIATION RELAY . 90	NORWEGIAN MOUNTAIN MARCH 135
SHUTTLE STEPPING STONES 91	OH, JOHNNY 136

8

OH! SUSANNA 137
OLD DAN TUCKER 138
POLKA 139
POP GOES THE
    WEASEL (SQUARE) 140
POP GOES THE WEASEL 141
RIGHT-HAND LADY WITH
    THE RIGHT-HAND GENT ... 143
SCHOTTISCHE COUPLE DANCE . 145
SCHOTTISCHE FOURSOME 146
SCHOTTISCHE STEP 147
SEVEN JUMPS 148
THREAD FOLLOWS THE NEEDLE 150
TROIKA 152
TWO-STEP 153
WALTZ 153

SAFETY ON THE PLAY-
    GROUND 154

Teach Safety to Children ... 154

Use of Apparatus 155

On the Ball Field 161

In Tag Games 162

In the Gym 162

In the Locker Room 162

Jungle Gym, Climbing
    Tower, Castle Tower, and
    Climbing Maze Games 163

TEAM GAMES 165

Teaching of Skills 166

SOCCER 167

Modified Soccer 167

Modified Soccer for Girls 172

Soccer Technique and Funda-
    mentals 177

Drills 186

CIRCLE DRIBBLE DRILL 186
PASS AND TRAP DRILL 187
SOCCER DRILLS 187

THROW-IN, HEAD,
    PASS, AND TRAP DRILL 188

Lead-Up Games 189
CIRCLE KICK 189
KICK BALL 190
LINE SOCCER 192
LONG BASE SOCCER 193
PIN SOCCER 194
SOCCER PUNT 195

Relays 196
FOOT DRIBBLE RELAY 196
SHUTTLE DRIBBLE RELAY 197
SOCCER PASS RELAY 198
THROW-IN FOR DISTANCE RELAY 199
ZIGZAG DRIBBLE RELAY 200

BASKETBALL 201

Basketball for Boys 202
Basketball Technique 208
Simplified Basketball for Girls 216

Drills 217
BASKETBALL
    DRIBBLE AND PIVOT 217
CIRCLE SHOOTING DRILL 218
DRIBBLE, LAY-UP,
    AND REBOUND DRILL 218
DRIBBLE PASS 220
FIVE ROUNDS 221
MEET-THE-BALL-
    AND-PASS DRILL 221
STOP DRILL 222
TRIANGLE DRILL 223
ZIGZAG DRIBBLE DRILL 223
ZIGZAG PASSING
    AND CATCHING DRILL 224
Lead-Up Games 224
NINE-COURT BASKETBALL 225
ONE-BASKET BASKETBALL 225

SOFTBALL 227

Basic Fundamental Skills and
    Techniques for Softball ... 235

Drills 241

BATTING AND
    BASE RUNNING DRILLS 241
OVERHAND THROW
    FOR ACCURACY DRILLS 242
UNDERHANDED PITCH DRILL . . 244
ZIGZAG THROW
    AND CATCH DRILLS 245

Lead-Up Games 245

BAR KICK BASEBALL 245
BAT BALL 246
BEAT THE BALL 247
LONG BALL 248
TEE BALL 249
Relays 250
BASE RUNNING RELAY 250
DIAMOND RELAY 251
GROUNDERS RELAY 252

HARDTOP GAMES 253

FOUR SQUARES BALL 253
HOME HOPSCOTCH OR SNAIL . . 254
HOPSCOTCH 255
JACKSTONES WITH BALL 259
LOOP TENNIS 263
ROLY POLY 263
TETHER BALL 265

GOAL GAMES 267

ANIMAL CHASE 267
ATTACK THE GOAL 268
BLACK AND WHITE 269
BOUNCE BALL 270
CALL THE NUMBER 271
CAPTURE THE FLAG 271
CROWS AND CRANES 273

DARE BASE 273
END BALL 275
FISH NET 276
FOUR SQUARE DODGE BALL 277
GUARD BALL 278
HIT THE FLOOR 278
KEEP AWAY 279
KICK-OFF TAG FOOTBALL 280
NOBBIES 281
PEE WEE 283
PRISONER'S BASE 284
REVENUE RUNNERS 286
RODEO 287
SLAP AND RUN 288
STEALING STICKS 289
STORM THE CASTLE 290

STUNTS: TUMBLING,
    PYRAMIDS, AND LOW
    BAR ACTIVITIES 291

General Hints 292
FORWARD ROLL 293
BACKWARD ROLL
    (FROM STANDING POSITION) . 294
BACKWARD ROLL
    (FROM SQUAT POSITION) . . 295
ASSIST SOMERSAULT 295
LEG ROCKER 296
ROCKER 297
HANDSTAND 297
SQUAT HAND BALANCE 298
NECK AND ELBOW BALANCE . . . 298
ASSIST HEADSTAND 299
TWO- OR THREE-MAN PYRAMID 299
HANDSTAND WITH PARTNER . . 300
THREE- OR FIVE-PIECE PYRAMID 301

BIBLIOGRAPHY 302

CHARACTERISTICS OF THE INTERMEDIATE AGE GROUP

Intermediate age boys and girls are interested in becoming members of a group or a team. Natural development helps to increase their skills; as their hands become larger, they are better able to handle balls, and, as their muscles become more coordinated, they can run, jump, and turn with greater ease. Girls can frequently out-run, out-play, and out-perform boys at this age. During this time, it is necessary to provide such lead-up games as soccer, softball and basketball, and such goal games as Capture the Flag, Prisoner's Base, Dodge Ball and Four Squares that involve both individual and team play. Since most of their activity is in vigorous games, the children's real interest lies in the basic motor skills of running, dodging, turning, stopping, throwing, climbing, and swimming. These are the activities for which they have natural ability, and developing skill in them through practice in the simple team games or lead-up games will provide the skills necessary in the more complicated team sports. These lead-ups are games in themselves, and they hold the intermediate group's interest because they are competitive, challenging, and much more suited to their physical and mental capacity.

Perfection of body coordination is not yet possible, but this is the stage of development when practice must begin if special and unusual skills are ever to be attained. Some coaching can be done at this period. Children can be taught the correct hold on a bat, the proper balance for throwing, and the development of rhythm in motion. This is the most opportune time for corrections, since movements have not yet become mechanical and natural to them.

At the lower intermediate age, children's imagination is still very vivid; as they reach the upper intermediate grades, however, they leave behind the world of make-believe in search of something real. Their comprehension widens, and they become interested in seasonal sports. They have a greater desire to belong to a group, and they become more willing to conform to group standards. They are also hungry for adult praise of their abilities and skills in activities; here the parent, teacher or coach can play an important role in encouraging the less matured and poorly skilled children by giving them special attention and tactful suggestions. Such attention will prevent

11

your program from bogging down with children not interested in physical education activities. As the school year develops, "horse-play" and inattention in the group will remain at a minimum.

Boys and girls are usually able to participate in the same activities within their own age groups. There is a gradual drawing away of the boys and girls from each other in the late intermediate grades; boys become more interested in individual, pair, and group games, while the girls prefer less rough activities. But we find that the boys and girls have not altogether lost interest in each other, for at this phase of development, they are going through the slapping, chasing, pushing and teasing stage. Boys adopt an attitude of rudeness and roughness toward all girls to display their masculine superiority.

The boys develop a greater sense of group responsibility and become highly critical of each other for mistakes and errors committed in team activities; the less skilled receive most of the abuse and criticism. At this age, they are more willing to learn skill activities. They are also interested in individual competition that lets them compete against single individuals, e.g., badge tests or even their own records. Many children of this age develop a desire to collect; they fill their pockets and their rooms with such odds and ends as bottle tops, stamps, match folders, marbles, string, ribbons, butterflies, and often, to the mother's distress, small bugs, mice, and other pet animals.

Boys and girls vary in their interests at the end of this period. The boys become more concerned with team play, while the girls devote their attention to folk and social dancing, dramatic expression, and adventure and romantic stories. Constructively, boys build model airplanes, boats, and automobiles, and bird houses. Boys and girls do some drawing, but the large leg and arm muscles are better developed than the smaller muscles of the hands and fingers. Their pictures become smaller and show better workmanship, although the absence of people is noticeable. Figures are difficult to draw, and their eye is seldom satisfied with the work of their hands; an eraser is frequently used more than a pencil. Often they will refuse to draw, saying they cannot do it. They thus need much encouragement and instruction.

During the period starting with ten years of age, the girls experience a rapid period of growth marked by decided physical and emotional changes; the boys usually follow a similar pattern one or two years later. This development is accompanied by fast growth of the long bones, and, as a result, there is a tendency toward awkwardness and poor posture. This is an age in which endurance decreases and

12

there is danger of over-fatigue. Parental pressures and domination are often resisted and rebelled against.

It is particularly important for leaders working with children in this age group to be well acquainted with and constantly aware of the many intricate characteristics which are demonstrated in the group activities. A lack of understanding on the leader's part may cause individual complexes to develop; these may have injurious effects on individuals or on an entire group, and may subsequently lead to disciplinary problems.

SUGGESTIONS

1. The presence of a leader in a play area encourages better discipline and order.
2. If a play area is well supervised, many of the minor problems and defects are settled by the children themselves.
3. Always maintain and encourage the spirit of justice, loyalty, and fair play.
   a) Never be lax about rules concerning the play area or the games.
   b) Don't be strict with one child and lenient with another.
   c) In a disciplinary case, try to learn all the facts before you act; poor planning and organization may have contributed to the lack of interest of the child or children in the activity, thus causing the problem.
4. Do not make threats or promises that you cannot or do not intend to carry out; such inconsistency weakens the respect of children for leadership ability.
5. The power of suggestion works miracles if used at the right time.

PREPARATION AND PLANNING

1. Encourage children to help in the planning.
   a) Permit them to choose games.
   b) Encourage them to introduce variations to old games.
   c) Be open to suggestions for rule changes.
2. Keep your program well-balanced.
   a) Folk dances and rhythms.
   b) Tag, circle, goal games, and relays.
   c) Team games.
   d) Individual stunts, tests, and activities.
3. Organize your program to include both boys and girls.

a) Boys and girls should learn to play together.

b) Activities planned for groups of boys and groups of girls should be conducted in the playfield where they will not interfere with each other.

4. Do not introduce too many new games in a short period of time; as a rule children enjoy playing one or two games in a play period. Choose a game, new or old, that will meet the needs and desires of the children.

5. Encourage informal and self-organized activities during play periods before school, during the noon hour, and after school.

6. Make your program progressive by using preliminary games before introducing the more complicated team games.

7. Prepare a well-organized lesson plan which will be flexible enough to provide for such changing conditions as weather, play area, and indoor facilities. Don't get into a "rut" by playing the same games day after day without introducing new games or variations to old ones.

8. Adjust games with a large number of players.

a) In tag games, increase the number of runners and chasers.

b) In circle games, make two or more circles.

c) In goal and team games, organize more groups.

d) In relays, add more files or use shuttle relays.

LEADER'S EVALUATION OF THE ACTIVITY PERIOD

1. Was the period well planned?

a) Were the games well chosen for the group?

b) Did the children enter wholeheartedly into the activities?

c) Did all the children have an opportunity to participate?

d) Were the activities safe?

e) Did the children have an opportunity to make suggestions for variations in the games and the rules?

f) Were basic skills taught?

g) Did the leaders assume responsibility?

h) Was good sportsmanship shown by obeying the rules and the official's decisions, and by following the leader's suggestions?

i) Was the game or drill enjoyed?

   (1) Was it work or fun?

   (2) Did the children understand the rules and skills of the activity?

FORMATIONS

1. Line or file formation (as diagramed): players stand in a straight line, facing the instructor.

2. Tandem formation (as diagramed): players stand in a double file.

LINE FORMATION

TANDEM FORMATION

3. Zigzag formation (as diagramed):
   a) In the activity or game to be played, every other player steps out as many steps as necessary.
   b) In some games and drills, the players face each other.
   c) In some games, each line represents a team.

4. Horseshoe formation (as diagramed):
   a) Players stand in a semi-circle formation.
   b) The leader stands in the center of the semi-circle.

ZIGZAG FORMATION

HORSESHOE FORMATION

5. Circle formation (as diagramed):
   a) Players stand in a circle.
   b) All players may face in or out, or may alternate, one facing inward and the next outward.
   c) Players may hold hands.

6. Double circle or concentric circle (as diagramed):
   a) Players may stand side-by-side in pairs.
   b) Players may face each other.
   c) Players may stand back-to-back.
   d) Players may face inward or outward.
   e) Players may form a circular zigzag pattern.

CIRCLE FORMATION   DOUBLE CIRCLE

7. Pair formation (as diagramed): this is usually used in pair relay games.

8. Shuttle relay formation (as diagramed): each team is divided into two groups which are placed at opposite ends of the playing area.

PAIR FORMATION   SHUTTLE FORMATION

TAG GAMES

ANTE I OVER

PLAYING FIELD: Any area with a shed, garage, or woodpile.

EQUIPMENT: Tennis ball, rubber ball, or sponge ball.

NUMBER OF PLAYERS: 6–30.

FORMATION: See diagram.

RULES OF THE GAME: Divide the group into 2 equal teams. The teams take their places on opposite sides of the building. Team "A" calls, "ANTE I OVER," and throws the ball over the building. Team "B" players try to catch the ball. If they succeed in catching the ball, they run around the building, and the player with the ball attempts to hit a player on team "A." Team "A" players try to get away by running around the opposite end of the building. If a player is hit, he joins the thrower's team.

If the ball is not caught, the team calls, "ANTE I OVER," and throws the ball back over the building to the opposite team.

If the ball should not go all the way over, the throwing team calls, "Pig Tail," and throws again.

The team wins that has the most players at the end of the play period.

17

ANTE I OVER

BALL TAG

PLAYING FIELD:	Gymnasium, playroom, or playfield.
EQUIPMENT:	Rubber playground ball, soccer ball, or rubber basketball.
NUMBER OF PLAYERS:	10–40.
FORMATION:	See diagram.

RULES OF THE GAME: One player is chosen to be "It." More may be chosen if a large group is playing. One "It" for each 10 players is suggested. The ball is passed from one player to another, and "It" tries to tag that player with the ball. If "It" tags a player while he is in possession of the ball, the two exchange places. If "It" intercepts the ball being passed, he exchanges places with the passer.

BALL TAG

BASE EXCHANGE

PLAYING FIELD:	Playground, gymnasium, or play-room.
EQUIPMENT:	8″ or 10″ rubber playground ball or volleyball. Bases made of any available material; e.g., cardboard cut in 10″ squares.
NUMBER OF PLAYERS:	5–40.
FORMATION:	See diagram.

RULES OF THE GAME: One player is chosen to be "It." All other players are on a base. "It" must hit a player with the ball when he is off base to get his base; the player hit then becomes "It." "It" may also steal an unoccupied base and the player left out becomes "It." If a player is "It" more than 2 minutes, the leader can call, "All Exchange," giving "It" a chance to get to a base, thus keeping the game active.

For 5–20 players, 1 "It" should be enough to produce an active game, but for more than 20, two can be chosen.

BASE EXCHANGE

BASE TAG

PLAYING FIELD:	Playground, gymnasium, or playroom.
EQUIPMENT:	Chalk or cardboard.
NUMBER OF PLAYERS:	10–40.
FORMATION:	See diagram.

RULES OF THE GAME: For the base markers use cardboard or draw chalk circles on the floor. One player will be "It." When "It" leaves his base, all players must leave their bases and seek new ones. "It" attempts to tag one of the players off base. No player may return to a base until he has occupied 3 other bases.

For a large group have 2 or more "Its."

BEANBAG HOP TAG

PLAYING FIELD:	Gymnasium, playroom, or playfield.
EQUIPMENT:	Beanbag.
NUMBER OF PLAYERS:	10–40.
FORMATION:	See diagram.

RULES OF THE GAME: Choose 1 "It" for every 10 players. "It" must carry a beanbag on his head; all other players must hop on one foot to keep away from him.

"It" cannot touch the beanbag with his hands when he attempts to tag a hopper. The hopper must keep hopping on the same foot he starts out with while being chased. If he changes feet or touches the other foot to the ground during the chase, he must exchange places with "It."

20

BEANBAG HOP TAG

CATCH THE PHEASANT

PLAYING FIELD:	Gymnasium, playroom, or playfield.
EQUIPMENT:	None.
NUMBER OF PLAYERS:	20–40.
FORMATION:	See diagram.

RULES OF THE GAME: Divide the group into equal teams, and arrange the teams in two separate lines. "A" line becomes the Foxes and "B" line the Pheasants. The player on the left end of the Pheasant line starts the game. On a signal, the Pheasant starts running for the other end of the line. He must run through each line at least 3 times, and the Fox must take the same route following him. If the Fox overtakes and tags the Pheasant, the Fox team receives 1 point; if the Pheasant escapes, his team gets the point.

CATCH THE PHEASANT

The first Fox and Pheasant take positions at the foot of their respective lines, and the game continues with the head couple starting out at the signal. After each player has had a turn, the teams reverse positions, the Pheasants acting as the Foxes, and Foxes as the Pheasants.

Players in the line cannot interfere with the runners, nor can the runners use their hands on the players in the line.

CHAIN TAG

PLAYING FIELD: Playground, gymnasium, or playroom.

EQUIPMENT: None.

NUMBER OF PLAYERS: 20–50.

FORMATION: See diagram.

RULES OF THE GAME: Two players are chosen "It." They join hands and attempt to tag the other players. When a player is tagged, he takes his place between the two ends and joins hands in the line. Only the end players may tag. When the chain surrounds a player, it is permissible for the player to break through or go under the joined hands of the line. When the chain has been broken, it must unite again before tagging is legal. The game is completed when the last player is caught or when a time limit is reached. The last 2 players caught act as "It" for the next game.

Boundary lines may be set up to restrict the play to a small area.

CHAIN TAG

EXCHANGE

PLAYING FIELD: Gymnasium, playroom, or playfield.
EQUIPMENT: None.
NUMBER OF PLAYERS: 20–50.
FORMATION: See diagram.

RULES OF THE GAME: Players pair off and hook elbows, boys with boys, girls with girls. One or two couples are chosen "It." "It" may roam around the playing area until he decides to call out, "Girls exchange," or, "Boys exchange." When "It" calls out, "Girls exchange," the girls must get a boy for a partner; on "Boys exchange," the boys must get a girl for a partner. On "All exchange," the girls must get a girl for a partner and the boys must get a boy for a partner. "It" attempts to tag one of the runners before he succeeds in hooking on to a partner. A runner who hooks on to the wrong partner can be tagged.

If "It" tags a runner, the runner becomes "It," and "It" pairs up with a partner, and the game continues.

EXCHANGE

23

HOOK ON

PLAYING FIELD: Playground, playroom, or gymnasium.

EQUIPMENT: None.

NUMBER OF PLAYERS: 10–40.

FORMATION: See diagram.

RULES OF THE GAME: One player acts as "It;" the other players form groups of 3 or 4, depending upon the size of the group. Standing in a file, one behind the other, each places his arms around the waist of the player in front. "It" tries to hook on the end of any file he can. The groups whip and twist around trying to protect the end of their group from being hooked, but they cannot break their file. If "It" hooks on to one of the groups, the leader of that group becomes "It."

For a large group of children have 2 or more "Its."

LAST COUPLE OUT

PLAYING FIELD: Playground, gymnasium, or playroom.

EQUIPMENT: None.

NUMBER OF PLAYERS: Any number.

FORMATION: See diagram.

RULES OF THE GAME: The players are arranged in a column, with couples standing together facing inward. One person who is "It" stands at the front of the column with his back to the other players. "It" calls, "Last couple out," and the last couple runs forward, one on either side of the line, in an attempt to join hands before "It" can tag them. "It" cannot look back or begin chasing until they are even with him. Should "It" tag one of the players, he

24

goes with the untagged person to the head of the line, and the person tagged is "It." If "It" misses, the couple goes to the head of the line, and the next couple comes out.

LAST COUPLE OUT

LIGHT NIGHT

PLAYING FIELD:	Gymnasium, playroom, or playfield.
EQUIPMENT:	None.
NUMBER OF PLAYERS:	10–40.
FORMATION:	See diagram.

RULES OF THE GAME: Divide players equally into 2 teams called "Lights and Nights." To identify the teams:

1. Roll up shirt sleeves of one team.
2. Tie a cloth to the arm of players of one team.
3. Have colored shirts vs. print shirts, or T-shirts vs. dress shirts.
4. Have tucked-in shirts vs. pulled-out shirts.

Have the teams scatter over the playing area. When the leader calls out "Lights," the "Lights" try to tag the "Nights," and vice versa.

To keep from being tagged, the players may choose a method before the game begins; e.g., hands on head, sitting on floor, etc. (See Safety Tags.) When a player is tagged, he is eliminated from the game. When one team has been eliminated, the other team has won the game.

LIGHT NIGHT

MYSTERY TAG

PLAYING FIELD: Gymnasium, playroom, or playfield.
EQUIPMENT: None.
NUMBER OF PLAYERS: 20–50.
FORMATION: See diagram.

MYSTERY TAG

RULES OF THE GAME: Divide the players into two equal groups which may be called "A's" and "B's," or "Dogs and Cats," or "Whales and Sharks." Each team lines up on its own goal line, and, on a signal, starts walking toward the center line. When they approach the center line, the leader calls "A," and "B's" chase the "A" team to its base. If one of the "A" players is tagged, he becomes a member of the "B" team. The game continues until the end of the play period, when the group having the most players is declared the winner.

Variation: Teams walk backward to the center line.

SAFETY TAGS

PLAYING FIELD:	Gymnasium, playroom, or playfield.
EQUIPMENT:	None.
NUMBER OF PLAYERS:	10–40.
FORMATION:	See diagram.

RULES OF THE GAME: When a player once breaks his safety position, he must run 10 steps before he may assume it again. "It" attempts to tag a player when he is not in a safety position. Before the game begins, the players must agree on the safety tag to be used.

The following safety tags are merely suggestions; groups may originate their own.

Players may be considered safe when they are:

1. Back to back with another player.
2. Grasping the ankles of another player.

3. Kneeling on one knee with arms outstretched.
4. Kneeling with the head touching the ground.

27

5. Kneeling on both knees, arms crossed, left hand holding right ear, right hand holding left ear.
6. Singing loudly, or reciting a poem or nursery rhyme.
7. Sitting upright with arms folded.

5.   6.   7.

8. Sitting with legs spread and touching the toes with the hands.
9. In a squat position, with the back straight and the arms folded or outstretched overhead.
10. Standing in the shadow of another player.
11. Standing on one foot.

8.   9.   10.   11.

12. Standing on one foot and touching the ground with one hand.
13. Touching the ground without bending knees.
14. Standing with legs crossed and hands on top of the head.

12.   13.   14.

SHOULDER TAG

PLAYING FIELD:	Gymnasium, playroom, or playfield.
EQUIPMENT:	None.
NUMBER OF PLAYERS:	10–40.
FORMATION:	See diagram.

RULES OF THE GAME: One player is chosen to be "It;" other players scatter over the playing area. "It" clasps hands behind his back and may tag only with his shoulders.

SHOULDER TAG

X **SNATCH THE HANDKERCHIEF**

PLAYING FIELD:	Gymnasium, playground, or playroom.
EQUIPMENT:	Handkerchief.
NUMBER OF PLAYERS:	Any number.
FORMATION:	See diagram.

RULES OF THE GAME: Two equal teams line up facing each other 5 yards or more apart. A handkerchief is placed in the center of the playing space between the two lines. Players in each line have corresponding numbers. The leader calls a number, and the 2 players holding that number go after the handkerchief. The player that is not successful in getting the handkerchief chases his opponent back, trying to tag him. One point is scored for the player returning safely to his line with the handkerchief.

20' TO 30'

SNATCH THE HANDKERCHIEF

PLAYING FIELD: Playground, gymnasium, or playroom.

EQUIPMENT: 8" rubber playground ball, chalk or cardboard bases.

NUMBER OF PLAYERS: 10–40.

FORMATION: See diagram.

SOCK "EM" BASE TAG

RULES OF THE GAME: Distribute the bases throughout the playing area, with the number of bases equal to the number of players. One player is designated as "It" and is given the ball. When "It" leaves his base, all players must exchange bases. A player cannot go back to his original base until he has stopped at 3 other bases. As the players run for other bases, "It" tries to hit one of them with the ball. If a player is hit, he becomes "It."

For a large group, have 2 or 3 "Its," one acting as the leader. When the leader steps off the base, the others scurry around the area, trying to hit a player who is off base.

PLAYING FIELD: Gymnasium, playroom, or playfield.
EQUIPMENT: 10″ rubber playground ball.
NUMBER OF PLAYERS: 10–40.
FORMATION: See diagram.

SPOT TAG

RULES OF THE GAME: One player is chosen to be "It." Start the game from a small circle in the center of the playing area. "It" is in the small circle, and the other players have one foot on the circle. While "It" bounces the ball twice, the players scatter to various parts of the playing area. "It" attempts to strike a player by throwing the ball at him, thus making him a "Spot." When a player becomes a "Spot," he is not allowed to move from that place, and he becomes an assistant to "It" and throws the ball at other players. "It" must recover the ball whenever it is not within reach of a "Spot," or before a "Spot" is made. He may pass the ball to a "Spot" or return to the center circle and throw at some player. This game must be played in a limited area, and is continued until all but one have become "Spots." The person who was not caught becomes "It" for the new game.

31

SQUARE TAG

PLAYING FIELD: Playground, playroom, or gymnasium.

EQUIPMENT: None.

NUMBER OF PLAYERS: 20–40.

FORMATION: See diagram.

40' TO 60'

40' TO 60'

SQUARE TAG

RULES OF THE GAME: Divide the players into 4 equal groups. Line a team up on each side of a large square and select one player from each team to be "It." The "It" players go to the middle of the square, and on a signal, the leader calls out one of the 4 team numbers. The players on that team run to the opposite base line. The "Its" in the center, except the "It" of the team called, try to tag the runners as they pass through the square. All players tagged join the tagger's team.

The leader continues to call team numbers until all players have had an opportunity to participate. New "Its" are chosen the second time around.

At the end of the play period the team having the most players wins the game.

STATUE TAG

PLAYING FIELD:	Playground, gymnasium, or playroom.
EQUIPMENT:	None.
NUMBER OF PLAYERS:	10–40.
FORMATION:	See diagram.

STATUE TAG

RULES OF THE GAME: Select one player to be "It"; the other players scatter about the designated area. "It" strikes a pose. Each player may strike this pose once to keep from being tagged, but after he has once taken the pose, he cannot take it again. He may hold the pose as long as he wishes.

Each "It" may have his own pose.

ZOO TAG

PLAYING FIELD: Playground, gymnasium, or play-room.

EQUIPMENT: None.

NUMBER OF PLAYERS: 10–40.

FORMATION: See diagram.

ZOO TAG

RULES OF THE GAME: Select a player to be the Zoo Keeper; the others are the animals. Each player who is to be an animal chooses from a list of 10 or 12 animals the animal he would like to be. The Zoo Keeper is placed on one base line and the animals line up on the opposite base. The Zoo Keeper calls out the name of an animal, and all players with this name run to the Zoo Keepers base line and back to the Zoo. At the same time the Zoo Keeper runs to the middle of the field and attempts to tag the animals before they can reach the Zoo. If he succeeds in tagging an animal, the tagged player becomes the Zoo Keeper, and the Zoo Keeper takes the name of one of the animals.

If the Zoo Keeper fails to tag an animal, he calls out the name of another animal. After a player has been called, he may change his animal name.

CIRCLE GAMES

BEAT THE COUNT

PLAYING FIELD: Gymnasium, playroom, or playground.

EQUIPMENT: Basketball, softball, soccer ball, or rubber playground ball.

NUMBER OF PLAYERS: 20–40.

FORMATION: See diagram.

RULES OF THE GAME: Divide the players into 2 teams. At a given signal, "A" team starts passing the ball around the circle. On each pass, the receiver calls out the count, 1–2–3–4, etc. Also on the signal, "B" team's leader runs around the "A" circle and touches his number 2 player, who in turn runs around; this continues until all "B" team has run around "A" team. When the last player in "B" team touches the leader, the latter calls out, "Stop the count," and "A" players stop at the last number called. Then the "A" and "B" teams exchange places. The game is started again with "B" passing and counting and "A" running around "B."

The team that has the highest total count in passing the ball wins the contest.

35

BEAT THE COUNT

BIRD, BEAST, OR FISH

PLAYING FIELD: Gymnasium, playground, playroom, or classroom.

EQUIPMENT: Sponge ball or 6″ rubber playground ball.

NUMBER OF PLAYERS: Any number.

FORMATION: See diagram.

BIRD, BEAST, OR FISH

RULES OF THE GAME: As a player in the center of the circle throws the ball to one of the players in the circle, he says quickly, "Bird, beast, or fish," and then repeats one of the words, e.g., "Bird," and immediately counts to 10. The receiver of the ball must name a bird and throw the ball back to the thrower before the latter reaches 10. Should the player with the ball fail to name the bird within the interval of the count, he changes places with the thrower, and the game continues.

Variation: No 2 players may call the name of the same bird, beast, or fish.

CIRCLE EXCHANGE TAG

PLAYING FIELD: Classroom, playroom, or gymnasium.
EQUIPMENT: None.
NUMBER OF PLAYERS: Any number.
FORMATION: See diagram.

RULES OF THE GAME: "It" is chosen, and all other players are numbered. "It" may roam around the room until the leader calls the numbers of 2 people. The 2 people called must exchange seats before "It" can get one of their vacant seats; the player left without a seat becomes "It."

If desks are in the room, "It" stands at the front of the classroom.

CIRCLE KEEP AWAY

PLAYING FIELD: Playground, gymnasium, or play-
                        room.

EQUIPMENT: Basketball, soccer ball, or volleyball.

NUMBER OF PLAYERS: 20–30.

FORMATION: See diagram.

RULES OF THE GAME: The game is played with "Keep Away" rules. Choose a player to be "It"; he takes his place in the circle. On a given signal, the players in the circle pass the ball around and across the circle; "It" tries to intercept the ball. If "It" is successful, the player passing the intercepted ball must exchange places with him. The game then continues with the new "It."

CIRCLE RACE

PLAYING FIELD: Playground, gymnasium, or play-
                        room.

EQUIPMENT: None.

NUMBER OF PLAYERS: 20–40.

FORMATION: See diagram.

RULES OF THE GAME: Players form a circle, each one an arm's length from the next; all face right. At a signal they begin to run, attempting to pass on the outside the person directly in front. If a person is passed, he drops to the center of the circle. Direction may be reversed at a signal also. The last player left is the winner.

CIRCLE RACE

CIRCLE STRIDE BALL

PLAYING FIELD: Playground or gymnasium.

EQUIPMENT: Any large ball.

NUMBER OF PLAYERS: Any number. Boys.

FORMATION: See diagram.

RULES OF THE GAME: Players stand with feet wide apart in a circle. "It" stands in the center of the circle with the ball and attempts to throw it through the spread legs of someone. Players must keep their hands on their knees until the ball leaves "It's" hands.

CIRCLE STRIDE BALL

CIRCLE TANTALIZERS

PLAYING FIELD: Gymnasium, playroom, or playfield.

EQUIPMENT: None.

NUMBER OF PLAYERS: 10–30.

FORMATION: See diagram.

RULES OF THE GAME: "It" squats in a 3 foot circle in the center of a 20–40 foot circle with all other players standing within the

CIRCLE TANTALIZERS

larger circle. Players tantalize "It," feinting as if they were going to touch him. "It" jumps up and chases the Tantalizers, who flee to safety outside the large circle.

When tagged, a Tantalizer becomes "It," and the game continues.

CIRCLE TARGET

PLAYING FIELD: Playground or gymnasium.

EQUIPMENT: Rubber play ball, basketball, or volleyball.

NUMBER OF PLAYERS: 20–40.

FORMATION: See diagram.

RULES OF THE GAME: Team "A" forms an inner circle about 15–20 feet in diameter. Team "B" forms an outside circle around team "A." The outside circle should be formed about 15–20 feet away from the inside circle.

Team "B" places one of its men within the team "A" circle, and attempts to get the ball to its man through team "A." Members of team "A" may kick or bat the ball away to prevent the center man from securing it, but they are not allowed to catch the ball. A member of team "B" may recover the ball from any spot on the play area but must return to his regular position to throw.

A team scores five points each time the ball is passed to its center man safely.

Time the game, giving each team 3 or 4 minutes to make a score, and then alternate positions.

CIRCLE
TARGET

END DODGE BALL

PLAYING FIELD:	Gymnasium, playroom, or playfield (Circle 30'–50').
EQUIPMENT:	Rubber playground ball.
NUMBER OF PLAYERS:	Any number.
FORMATION:	See diagram.

RULES OF THE GAME: Four players are chosen to play in the center of the circle. They stand in a line, each placing his hands around the waist of the player in front. On a given signal, the players standing on the circle pass the ball around the ring trying to get it in position to hit the player at the end of the line. As each player is hit, he joins the circle. When all players have been hit, a new group goes to the middle of the ring.

For large groups make more circles and have 2 or more games being played at the same time.

GENERAL AND HIS MEN

PLAYING FIELD: Gymnasium, playroom, or playfield.
EQUIPMENT: 8″ rubber playground balls.
NUMBER OF PLAYERS: 20–60.
FORMATION: See diagram.

RULES OF THE GAME: Divide the players into equal teams. Four men from the opposing team are placed within each circle. One of the 4 is known as the General. Each team has a rubber playground ball, and at a given signal the players in the circle try to hit the Men within the circle. The General in each circle tries to ward off the ball with his hands, feet or body to keep his Men from being hit; he may not catch the ball. The Men try to dodge the balls thrown at them; if hit, they are eliminated. The players in the circle may recover the ball within the circle, but must return to the circle to throw. The first circle to eliminate its Men wins. The leader appoints 4 players from each circle to start new games; each time, one of the 4 is appointed the General. The circle winning the most games wins the contest.

25′ TO 30′

GENERAL AND HIS MEN

JUNGLE CHIEF

> PLAYING FIELD: Playground, gymnasium, or playroom.
>
> EQUIPMENT: None.
>
> NUMBER OF PLAYERS: 20–40.
>
> FORMATION: See diagram.

RULES OF THE GAME: Select one player to act as Jungle Chief. The Chief sits in a circle 40 or 50 feet from the base line. Select one player to act as the Guide. All of the remaining players line up behind the base line, which is 40–50 feet long.

On a signal, the Guide goes behind the line tapping as many players on the back as he wishes; these players form a line behind him for an expedition. When the Guide has sufficient players for the expedition, he proceeds to the Jungle Chief. The expedition forms a circle around the Jungle Chief and does any type of dance. When the Chief claps his hands, they all stop in place. Then the Guide stamps his foot, and they all run for the base line. On the same signal, the Jungle Chief jumps up and chases the players. If he fails to tag one before they reach the base line, he remains the Chief, and the Guide picks a new group. If the Chief is successful and tags a player, the tagged player becomes the Chief and the old Chief becomes the Guide.

LAME FOX AND CHICKENS

> PLAYING FIELD: Gymnasium, playroom, or playfield.
>
> EQUIPMENT: None.
>
> NUMBER OF PLAYERS: 10–30.
>
> FORMATION: See diagram.

43

LAME FOX AND CHICKENS

RULES OF THE GAME: The Fox stands in the circle. The other players, scattered about outside of the circle, are the Chickens, and they taunt the Fox with such expressions as "Lame Fox, Lame Fox, you can't catch me." At will, the Fox chases one of the Chickens. While he is within the circle, he may run, but while outside, he must hop. There are no goal lines for safety. The Fox may return to his circle if he is not able to tag one of the Chickens. If he tags a Chicken, the latter becomes the Fox.

MAN IN THE CIRCLE

PLAYING FIELD: Gymnasium, playroom, or playfield.

EQUIPMENT: 10″ rubber playground ball, basketball, or volleyball.

NUMBER OF PLAYERS: 10–40.

FORMATION: See diagram.

RULES OF THE GAME: The center man has the ball; he passes it to any one of the players in the surrounding circle. The receiver throws the ball back to the center man, runs toward him, and tries to tag him. The center man must attempt to escape from the circle with the ball before being tagged by the circle chaser.

44

MAN IN THE CIRCLE

NUMBER PLEASE

PLAYING FIELD:	Gymnasium, playroom, playfield, or classroom.
EQUIPMENT:	None.
NUMBER OF PLAYERS:	10–20.
FORMATION:	See diagram.

RULES OF THE GAME: Players choose a number from 0–9; no one knows another player's number. One player in the circle says a number and then calls "Please." The players with the number called must exchange places; the center player tries to get to an opening before one of the exchanging players. If "It" does not secure a place, he calls 2 numbers; he adds numbers until he secures a place.

The player who is unsuccessful in securing a place in the circle is "It" the next time.

SKIP AROUND THE CIRCLE

PLAYING FIELD: Playground or gymnasium.
EQUIPMENT: None.
NUMBER OF PLAYERS: Any number.
FORMATION: See diagram.

SKIP AROUND
THE CIRCLE

RULES OF THE GAME: Players form a large circle with one person on the outside. The outside person is "It," and he must skip around and tag someone. The person tagged must skip in the opposite direction. When the two meet, they stop and bow, then link arms and skip a circle before continuing back to the vacant spot. The first one to reach the vacancy can have it; the other continues as "It."

SNAP THE TRAP

PLAYING FIELD:	Gymnasium, playroom, or playfield.
EQUIPMENT:	None.
NUMBER OF PLAYERS:	20–40.
FORMATION:	See diagram.

SNAP THE TRAP

STOP!

WEAVING

RULES OF THE GAME: Players form 2 circles, the inner circle having 4 to 16 players, depending upon the number of children participating in the game. The inner circle forms the trap. The players in the outer circle stand 10–20 feet away from the inner circle; they do not hold hands. On a given signal, the two circles start moving in opposite directions. For a second signal, the leader calls "Stop." The trap players lift their hands, and the Mice (outside circle) weave in and out of the trap.

The leader blows the whistle again and calls "Snap." The players in the inner circle drop their hands quickly, catching all Mice that are inside the trap. The prisoners join the trap, and the game continues until all Mice have been caught.

47

STORMY OCEAN

PLAYING FIELD:	Playground, gymnasium, or play-room.
EQUIPMENT:	Chalk.
NUMBER OF PLAYERS:	10–40.
FORMATION:	See diagram.

STORMY OCEAN

RULES OF THE GAME: Players divide into pairs, and each pair draws a circle in which to stand. The circles should be evenly scattered about the playing area. The couples in the circles choose the names of fish. One couple is without a circle, and they are called Tiger Sharks. As the Tiger Sharks move around the circles, they call names of fish. The couples whose fish names are called fall in behind the Tiger Sharks and follow them around the field. When the Tiger Sharks have called all the fish names they can think of, they say "Stormy Ocean," upon which all fish in the line run for an empty circle. The pair failing to secure a circle become the Tiger Sharks for the next game.

Variation: The Tiger Sharks could be called Whales.

48

Nature games add variety to the selection list, but considerable preparation is frequently necessary to insure a successful outcome. Many of these contests require the use of large collections of bird or animal pictures or of specimens of leaves, weeds, or flowers to be identified. Frequently a preliminary game may be designed for the purpose of gathering items which will be used in other contests.

For identification games, the leader must bear in mind that knowledge of nature is rather limited for most children of this age. Usually it is advisable to provide instruction in order to make the children familiar with the varieties or species to be used. This familiarization can easily be effected on the previous day in a schoolroom situation, and also can be made a game itself.

BIRD DESCRIPTION

PLAYING FIELD: Classroom, playground, country, or park.

EQUIPMENT: Make cards with written descriptions of birds on them.

NUMBER OF PLAYERS: 6–20.

FORMATION: See diagram.

RULES OF THE GAME: Read the description slowly and clearly so that all players are able to understand it, and then have players take turns guessing the bird described. The first player to identify the bird is given the card; anyone giving the wrong answer must give up a card. At the end of the game, the player with the most cards wins.

Suggestion: Give the class pictures and descriptions of birds to study before playing the game. Draw pictures of birds. Color mimeographed pictures of birds and write their description below the drawing.

DEER STALKING

PLAYING FIELD: Wooded area or park.
EQUIPMENT: None.
NUMBER OF PLAYERS: 10–30.
FORMATION: See diagram.

RULES OF THE GAME: Choose one of the players to act as the deer. He stands or moves about in a small area (10 foot circle) and does not hide. The other players scatter out and hide; at a given signal, they approach as close as possible to the Deer without being seen by him. If the Deer spots a player, he will ask the player to stand up. After a given period, the leader will signal "Time," and all players not detected will stand. The nearest undetected player wins the contest and becomes the Deer for the next game.

Variation: Blindfold the Deer, and spread dry twigs around the 10′ circle. Scatter the players at a distance of 100 feet from the Deer; at a signal, they try to sneak up on him. If the Deer hears a player approach, he points and calls, "Stop." If he points in the direction of an approaching player, that player is eliminated. The first player to touch the blindfolded deer wins the contest.

51

DUPLICATE

PLAYING FIELD: Playground, park, or camp.
EQUIPMENT: Leaves, wild flowers, and weeds.
NUMBER OF PLAYERS: 10–30.
FORMATION: See diagram.

DUPLICATE

RULES OF THE GAME: Give each player a leaf, wild flower, or weed. At a given signal, he must run out and find a duplicate and return to the leader. If he finds a correct duplicate, the leader will give the player another plant to find. Five points are scored for each duplicate found. The player with the most points wins the contest.

Variation: Divide the players into relay teams. Give each player a leaf, flower, or weed. At a given signal, the first player of each team starts out to find his duplicate. On finding a like object, he runs back to the leader to verify it. If correct, the next player of his team sets out. The first team to finish wins the contest.

Suggestion: To gather material for the contest, another game is suggested. At a given signal, players scatter to gather as many different leaves, wild flowers, or weeds as they can before the leader calls time. At a signal, the players check in their findings with the leader. The player with the greatest variety of leaves, flowers, or weeds wins the contest.

GETTING PARTNERS

PLAYING FIELD: Classroom or playground.

EQUIPMENT: Appropriate plant life and paper slips.

NUMBER OF PLAYERS: 10–30.

FORMATION: See diagram.

RULES OF THE GAME: The players search for their partners in the following situations:

1. Cut leaves in two, and distribute the halves among the players.
2. Give leaves to the boys and fruits to the girls.
3. Give questions to the boys and answers to the girls.
4. Give duplicate slips naming animals or birds to the boys and girls. The boys imitate the animal or bird by action or voice; the girls claim their partners by recognizing the imitations.
5. Use birds or animals; Mr. and Mrs. Crow, Canary, Owl, etc.
6. Have the players match silhouettes of trees or leaves.
7. Have the players match constellations.
8. Have the players match popular songs (eliminate the titles).

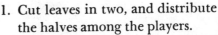

I SPY

PLAYING FIELD: Wooded area, park, or camp.

EQUIPMENT: Paper and pencils.

NUMBER OF PLAYERS: 5–15.

FORMATION: See diagram.

RULES OF THE GAME: The leader says, "I spy a tree," "I spy a flower," "I spy a bird," etc., whereupon each player writes down the name of the tree. The player giving the most correct answers wins the contest.

Variation: Divide the group into teams, with one player on each team acting as a recorder. Each team confers to decide upon the correct answer. When time is called, each team writes down its decision. The team with the greatest number of correct answers wins the contest.

LEAF RELAY

PLAYING FIELD: Playground, park, or wooded area.

EQUIPMENT: List of trees in the area for each group.

NUMBER OF PLAYERS: 10–30.

FORMATION: See diagram.

RULES OF THE GAME: Give the first player of each team a tree list. At a given signal, he hands the list to number two player and runs out to get a leaf of the first tree named. When he returns with the correct leaf, the number two player hands the list to number three and sets out to find his leaf. The first group to get all of the correct leaves wins the contest.

LEAF RELAY

MATCHING LEAVES

PLAYING FIELD:	Playground with trees.
EQUIPMENT:	Leaves.
NUMBER OF PLAYERS:	Any number.
FORMATION:	See diagram.

RULES OF THE GAME: Gather 10 or 15 leaves and cut them in half. Give each player half a leaf. He must find the matching half. When all players have matched their leaves, the partners must be able to tell what trees the leaves came from.

MATCHING LEAVES

NATURE ALPHABET

PLAYING FIELD:	School room, playground, or home.
EQUIPMENT:	None.
NUMBER OF PLAYERS:	10–15.
FORMATION:	See diagram.

RULES OF THE GAME: Nature categories such as flowers, birds, and animals are used in this game. In the bird category, the number one player calls out, "Name birds that start with the letter O." The player to his left names 1 bird, and the other players around the circle continue in sequence until the option returns to the first player. If he can name another bird whose name begins with the letter O, he receives 5 points. The game then continues with the leader calling out another letter of the alphabet. Each player who gives a correct name receives 1 point. The player who accumulates the most points wins the contest.

Suggested categories: Trees, birds, animals, leaves, flowers, rocks, stars, and weeds.

NATURE SPY

PLAYING FIELD:	Playground, park, or woods.
EQUIPMENT:	None.
NUMBER OF PLAYERS:	10–20.
FORMATION:	See diagram.

RULES OF THE GAME: All players sit in a large circle, and each in turn names a nature object which can be seen or heard at the time. When a player can not think of a new object, he leaves the circle. When half of the players have been eliminated, all remaining players divide into groups. The eliminated players are then divided

NATURE SPY

among these groups in which they act as hunters in finding nature objects for their side to use. Each time an object cannot be identified by the opposing team, the other team receives 1 point. The team with the most points at the end of the play period wins the contest.

PEEP HOLE

PLAYING FIELD: Classroom, playground, or home.

EQUIPMENT: Piece of cardboard, 18″ x 18″ with a 3″ hole in the center.

NUMBER OF PLAYERS: 10–30.

FORMATION: See diagram.

RULES OF THE GAME: The leader places leaves in the peep hole, and the players identify the leaves. One point is given for each correct answer.

Variation: Use pictures of birds, flowers, or animals. Divide the group into 2 equal teams, each taking a turn in identifying the object. The team with the most correct answers wins the contest.

PEEP HOLE

PINE BALL

PLAYING FIELD: Park, playground, or camp.

EQUIPMENT: Pine cones, or 6″ or 8″ rubber playground balls if pine cones are not available.

NUMBER OF PLAYERS: 12–30.

FORMATION: See diagram.

RULES OF THE GAME: Select 1 player from each side to be score keeper; the latter records the misses of the opposite team. Each team is given 3 balls or pine cones. At a given signal, the cones are thrown over a rope to the other team. If a cone is not caught and falls to the ground, the throwing team scores 1 point; if it is thrown out of bounds (20 feet back of the rope), the throw does not count, and the receiving team puts the cone back into play.

Time: four 4-minute quarters. Teams change sides at the end of each quarter. The team with the highest number of points wins the contest.

PINE BALL

SCAVENGER HUNT

PLAYING FIELD: Wooded area, park, or camp.
EQUIPMENT: None.
NUMBER OF PLAYERS: 10–30.
FORMATION: See diagram.

SCAVENGER HUNT

RULES OF THE GAME: The leader makes out lists of objects to be found in the area and gives the lists to the team captains. At a given signal, the teams set out to find the objects on the list.

The list of objects might include such things as types of leaves, flowers, bugs, rocks, moss, butterflies, ferns, weeds, grass, clay, four-leaf clovers, and seeds.

Variations: Gather objects whose names begin with different letters.

Another variation may be played with individuals competing for points. The search is for one article at a time from a list of 5 or 10 previously decided upon by the leader. Contestants must find the object (such as a pine cone, dandelion, or maple leaf) and return to the leader with it. Points may be given on a 5–3–1 basis or 5–4–3–2–1 basis, depending upon the number of contestants. The winner is the person with the highest point total at the end of the contest.

TRAILING

PLAYING FIELD:	Wooded area, park, or camp.
EQUIPMENT:	None.
NUMBER OF PLAYERS:	6–15.
FORMATION:	See diagram.

RULES OF THE GAME: Select a player to go through the woods and leave behind tell-tale marks as he travels by making scuff marks in the ground, breaking twigs and leaving them in the path, and placing rock and grass signs. After 10–15 minutes, send the players out to track their prey. The trailmarker should stop after 15 minutes of making signs and wait for the group to find him. To make the game more interesting, he should go off the main trails; he will thus draw his trackers off the usual courses and give them an opportunity to follow new paths.

The first player to find the trailmarker wins the contest and will be the trailmarker for the next game.

Variation: The game may also be designed as a time game; the interval from the beginning of the search until the prey is found determines the winner.

THE BELL RINGS

PLAYING FIELD: Classroom.

EQUIPMENT: Small bell.

NUMBER OF PLAYERS: 10–20.

FORMATION: See diagram.

RULES OF THE GAME: "It" closes his eyes and counts to 20 aloud. As he is counting, the bell is passed around the circle; as he approaches 20, everyone places his hands behind his back. As soon as "It" reaches 20, he opens his eyes and tries to guess who has the bell. All the contestants should act the same, "guilty or not guilty." If "It" succeeds in finding the bell, the player who was in possession of the bell must exchange places with him. If he fails, he must close his eyes again, and the procedure is repeated.

Suggestion: With a large group, have more than one "It."

61

THE BELL RINGS

BIRD, FLOWER, OR TREE

PLAYING FIELD: Classroom, playground, camp, or home.

EQUIPMENT: None.

NUMBER OF PLAYERS: 10–30.

FORMATION: See diagram.

RULES OF THE GAME: "It" points to a player and calls, "Tree." Before "It" can count to 10, the player must respond with the name of a tree; if "It" says "Flower," the player must respond with the name of a flower. Any player failing to answer within the count of 10 becomes "It."

Variation: "It" may call the name of a bird, flower, or tree to which the player must answer with the word "Bird," "Flower," or "Tree" before "It" counts to 5.

BIRDS FLY

PLAYING FIELD:	Classroom, gymnasium, playroom, or playfield.
EQUIPMENT:	None.
NUMBER OF PLAYERS:	20–40.
FORMATION:	See diagram.

RULES OF THE GAME: "It" takes his place in front of the group. The players in the group wave their arms like wings, for example, whenever "It" calls out the name of a bird. "It" may call out the names of animals, fish, or birds and wave his hands when he calls such phrases as "Dogs fly," "Chickens fly," "Lions fly," and "Trout fly." The group wave their arms when anything that can fly is called. Any player who waves his arms when a non-flyer is called, is eliminated.

The game continues until all but one is eliminated. He will be "It" for the next game.

BIRDS FLY

FRUIT OR VEGETABLE BASKET

PLAYING FIELD: Classroom.
EQUIPMENT: Chairs.
NUMBER OF PLAYERS: 12–30.
FORMATION: See diagram.

FRUIT OR VEGETABLE BASKET

RULES OF THE GAME: Players number off in 4's, 5's, 6's, 7's, or 8's, depending on the size of the group. Use names of fruit for each group, e.g., number 1, pineapples; number 2, lemons; 3, apples; 4, peaches; 5, plums. "It" is the vendor, who calls the name of one of the fruits. When he calls a fruit, everyone who belongs to that fruit must change places with some other person in the group. All other fruits remain in place. While the exchange is being made, the vendor tries to secure one of the vacant chairs or positions in the circle. If he is successful, the one who is left without a place becomes "It," and the game continues. Whenever he wishes, "It" may call, "Fruit basket upset," and everyone must exchange places.

Variation: Use vegetables, cities, or animals.

I AM A FARMER AND I KNOW MY STOCK

PLAYING FIELD: Classroom, gymnasium, or home.

EQUIPMENT: None.

NUMBER OF PLAYERS: 10–30.

FORMATION: See diagram.

RULES OF THE GAME: One player, appointed as the farmer, is blindfolded. He walks around the circle, points to someone in the circle, and says, "This is my pig." The player must answer by making a sound like a pig. The farmer tries to identify the player. If he guesses the player's name, they exchange places. If not, he continues around the circle. The farmer should be allowed 3 guesses.

MIMIC THE LEADER

PLAYING FIELD: Classroom, home, or gymnasium.

EQUIPMENT: None.

NUMBER OF PLAYERS: 10–30.

FORMATION: See diagram.

RULES OF THE GAME: "It" places his hands over his eyes, while the teacher or leader points to the player to act as the first group leader. Everyone in the circle is to mimic the leader. "It" tries to find who is the leader of the group. As "It" turns around, trying to find the leader, the leader changes his motion. He may use such motions as swinging arms, tapping feet, moving head, waving hands or feet, turning around, jumping, stamping, kneeling, and running. "It" watches the players until he thinks he knows who is the leader of the group. If he guesses correctly, they exchange places, if not, "It" continues until he has had 3 guesses. If he has not guessed the leader in 3 tries, the teacher or leader will appoint a member of the circle to take the place of "It."

OBJECT EXCHANGE

PLAYING FIELD: Classroom, gymnasium, playroom, or home.

EQUIPMENT: Beanbag, book, pencil, playground ball, eraser, and softball. If the group is large, extra articles may be placed in the circle.

NUMBER OF PLAYERS: 10–30.

FORMATION: See diagram.

RULES OF THE GAME: Start the equipment around the circle, and allow no player in the circle to hold more than 1 article at a time. As the articles are being passed from one player to the next, "It" may call out 2 items at any time he chooses, and the players who are in possession of these items must exchange places. While the players are exchanging, "It" tries to secure one of their places. If he succeeds, the one who is left without a place will be "It," and the game continues.

OBJECT EXCHANGE

PLAYING FIELD: Playroom, playfield, or classroom.

EQUIPMENT: A piece of string long enough to form a circle accommodating all of the players. Place a ring on the string and tie the ends together.

NUMBER OF PLAYERS: 10–40.

FORMATION: See diagram.

THE RING ON THE STRING

RULES OF THE GAME: Players sit or stand in a circle, holding the string, palms down. One or more players act as "Detectives" (the number depending upon the number of players). The players holding the string pass the ring from one to another. The "Detectives" in the middle attempt to find the ring; the players in the circle try to deceive them by moving the hands as if passing the ring. If a "Detective" thinks he has found the ring, he points to the hands of the suspected player. If he is correct, the two exchange places. If a detective makes 5 mistakes, he is discharged, and the last person accused of having the ring takes his place.

TEAM RELAYS

SHUTTLE RELAYS

RELAYS

PAIR RELAYS

LIMITED AREA RELAYS

RELAYS

In the physical education program, relays have a universal appeal which furnishes enjoyment and excitement for both boys and girls. In this type of activity, the children not only have fun, but they also develop strength, vigor, and endurance. Relays play an important part in the development of skills for other activities; they give all children an opportunity to compete. They help children socially, giving them a chance to play with others, to learn the spirit of fair play, to acquire desirable attitudes, to become loyal to a group, and to play according to a set of rules.

Relays can be adjusted to the age and the capacity of the group.

TEACHING TECHNIQUE HINTS

1. Divide players into equal teams.
2. Players fumbling or losing the object used in the relay must recover it and come back into line before the game continues.
3. After a player has completed his turn, he may sit, squat, or kneel on the floor, or he may hold his hands above his head; such indication will aid the judge to determine the winners.
4. Use a point system in scoring relays.
5. Suggestions for choosing teams:
   a) Count off by 2's, 3's, 4's, etc.
   b) Choose teams by colors (contestants select colored bands to determine teams).
   c) Captains choose teams.
   d) Line players up according to height, and have them count off. Number one steps forward and forms a relay line, two follows, etc.
6. Uneven teams.
   a) Have the first player in the line repeat the relay twice; he will then be at the end of the line for the second relay, and the number two player will repeat on the second relay.
   b) Have the tallest or shortest player of each team run twice, or appoint any one player to run twice.
7. Starting and turning lines should be well marked before a relay starts so that all players will understand the rules.
8. One method of starting players in a relay is to have the first player on each team run to the turning line and back. He must touch the second player on the hand or pass some object to him before the latter may run.

9. It is sometimes desirable to mark the last runner so that the judges can better decide the winners. A colored piece of cloth tied around the arm or tucked into the belt can designate the last man.

RELAY FORMATIONS

1. Court Relay Formation (as diagramed): The teams line up at each corner of the court.

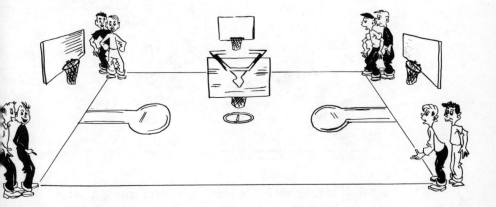

2. Spoke Relay Formation (as diagramed): the player files represent the spokes of a wheel.

BOUNCE RELAY

PLAYING FIELD: Gymnasium, playroom, or play-ground.

EQUIPMENT: Basketball or soccer ball.

NUMBER OF PLAYERS: 20–40.

FORMATION: See diagram.

RULES OF THE GAME: Divide each team into "A" and "B" groups. At a given signal, the first "A" player bounce-passes the ball to his "B" partner; "B" returns the ball to the next "A" player and the ball thus continues toward the end of the line. The last player in the line rolls the ball back to the starting player.

The team finishing first wins the relay.

DRIBBLE RELAY

PLAYING FIELD: Gymnasium, playroom, or play-ground.

EQUIPMENT: Basketballs.

NUMBER OF PLAYERS: 20–40.

FORMATION: See diagram.

DRIBBLE RELAY

RULES OF THE GAME: The first player of each team is given a ball, and at a given signal he dribbles the ball, weaves down the line between his teammates, goes around the last player, weaves back to his starting position, and throws the ball to the number two man. The latter does the same, but must go around the number one man and back to his position before throwing the ball to number three. The last man, after getting back to his position, rolls the ball back to the number one man.

ELEPHANT WALK RELAY

PLAYING FIELD:	Gymnasium, playroom, or playground.
EQUIPMENT:	None.
NUMBER OF PLAYERS:	20–40. Boys.
FORMATION:	See diagram.

ELEPHANT WALK RELAY

RULES OF THE GAME: The player must keep the knees straight and grasp the ankles with the hands. At a given signal, the player at the head of the line "elephant-walks" to the turning line and back to touch off the next player.

73

INDIAN CLUB RELAY

PLAYING FIELD: Gymnasium, playroom, or playground.

EQUIPMENT: Indian clubs or 2 by 4's, 2 feet long.

NUMBER OF PLAYERS: 20–40.

FORMATION: See diagram.

RULES OF THE GAME: At a given signal, the first player of each team runs to the Indian club, picks it up, runs back to the starting line, and places it on the ground in front of the next player's feet. The next player cannot run with the Indian club, however, until the club is balanced in an upright position. The number two player picks up the club, runs to the line, sets up the club in the same fashion, and then runs back to his team, sending off the next player.

The first team to complete the round wins.

INDIAN CLUB RELAY
20' TO 40'

LEAPFROG RELAY

PLAYING FIELD: Gymnasium, playroom, or playground.

EQUIPMENT: None.

NUMBER OF PLAYERS: 20–40. Boys.

FORMATION: See diagram.

74

LEAPFROG RELAY

FINISH
LINE

RULES OF THE GAME: Players bend over, placing hands on ankles. At a given signal, the last player starts leaping over his teammates by placing the palms of his hands on their backs. When he arrives at the head of the line, he assumes the bent leapfrog position.

As soon as a team member becomes the last man on the team, he proceeds to leap over his teammates. The team whose last man crosses the finish line first wins.

Variation: Leapfrog may be used as a shuttle relay by dividing the group into "A," "B," and "C" sections. The "A" section starts, and when they reach the "B" section, the "B's" leap down to the line the "A's" started from, and the "C's" come back to start the "A's" back to their original position. This continues until all teams are back into their original positions. The first team back in position wins the relay.

TURN
LINE

OBSTACLE RELAY

PLAYING FIELD: Playground, playroom, or gymnasium.

EQUIPMENT: Obstacles: benches, tires, hurdles, boxes, chairs, rolled mats, etc.

NUMBER OF PLAYERS: 16–40. Boys.

FORMATION: See diagram.

RULES OF THE GAME: Between the starting and the turning lines, place a series of obstacles in the path of each team. At a given signal, the first player of each team runs through the obstacles to the turning line, by jumping, stepping, or crawling past the obstacles in his path, and then returning through the obstacles again, and touching the next player in line.

The first team to reach its original position wins the relay.

Variation: This relay may be used as a shuttle relay. See shuttle relay formation.

ONE-HAND RELAY

PLAYING FIELD: Gymnasium, playroom, or playground.

EQUIPMENT: Basketball, beanbag, soccer ball, or eight-inch rubber playground ball.

NUMBER OF PLAYERS: 20–40.

FORMATION: See diagram.

RULES OF THE GAME: Players stand in line with their left hands behind their backs. The first player passes the ball to the next player, who must catch the ball and pass to the next player down the line. When the last player in the line receives the ball, he runs to the front of the line and passes to the number one player, who has moved back one position. A player fumbling or missing a pass must retrieve the ball with his right hand and come back to his position before passing the ball.

Variation: Use the left hand instead of the right.

ONE-HAND RELAY

OVERHEAD PASS RELAY

PLAYING FIELD:	Gymnasium, playroom, or playground.
EQUIPMENT:	Basketballs, soccer balls, or 8″ playground balls.
NUMBER OF PLAYERS:	20–40.
FORMATION:	See diagram.

RULES OF THE GAME: At a given signal, the number one player starts the game by passing the ball over his head to the next player; each player leaves his hands in the air after making the pass. When the ball gets to the end of the line, the last player starts the ball back to the front of the line by placing the ball into the hands of the player in front of him.

OVERHEAD PASS RELAY

Any ball dropped must be retrieved by the player dropping the ball, and he must get back into position before passing the ball to the next player.

Variation: Pass the ball between the legs.

PASS AND ZIGZAG RELAY

PLAYING FIELD: Gymnasium, playroom, or playground.

EQUIPMENT: Basketballs, volleyballs, soccer balls, or rubber playground balls.

NUMBER OF PLAYERS: 20–40.

FORMATION: See diagram.

RULES OF THE GAME: Divide the players into equal teams. At a given signal, the end player starts the ball down the line with a two-handed side pass. When the number one player receives the ball, he runs to the turning line and back, zigzags through his own line to the rear, and passes the ball to the next player in line. After each player makes his pass, he moves forward to the next position.

Any ball dropped or fumbled must be recovered by the guilty player, and he must return to his place in line before throwing the ball.

The first team to complete the cycle wins.

TURN LINE   ←8' TO 12'→

PRONE CIRCLE RELAY

PLAYING FIELD: Gymnasium, playroom, or playground.

EQUIPMENT: None.

NUMBER OF PLAYERS: 20–40. Boys.

FORMATION: See diagram.

PRONE CIRCLE RELAY

RULES OF THE GAME: The players lie face down, hands under face, elbows close to sides, feet straight back; each team lies in a circle. A head man is selected by each circle to start the game, and at a given signal, this man jumps up and runs around the circle, stepping over the legs of his teammates and back to his original position. As soon as the runner falls into a prone position, the next player jumps up and runs, until all have run. The first team to finish wins the relay.

RAIL BALANCE RELAY

PLAYING FIELD: Gymnasium, playroom, or playground.
EQUIPMENT: Two 2″ x 4″, 10′ long balance rails.
NUMBER OF PLAYERS: 20–40.
FORMATION: See diagram.

RULES OF THE GAME: At a given signal, the first player of each team walks the balance rail to the end, returns to his line, and tags the second player. If a player loses his balance and touches the floor, he must return to the start of the balance board and begin again. The team returning to its original position first wins the relay.

Variation:

EQUIPMENT: Add basketball.
FORMATION: Same as above.

RULES OF THE GAME: At a given signal, the first player of each team walks the balance board while dribbling a basketball on the floor. The player returns to his line by dribbling the ball and handing it to the next player. The game continues until all players have competed. The team to finish first wins the contest.

A RAINY WASH-DAY RELAY

PLAYING FIELD:	Gymnasium, playroom, or playground.
EQUIPMENT:	Skipping ropes, towels.
NUMBER OF PLAYERS:	20–40.
FORMATION:	See diagram.

RULES OF THE GAME: The first player of each team is given a gym towel. Two players from each team hold up the rope at the turn line. At a given signal, the first player of each team takes the towel to the line, places it over the line so that the bottom edges are even, and changes places with one of the clothes line holders. The latter turns back and touches the number two man, who removes the towel and takes it back to the next player; he hangs it on the rope and replaces one of the holders.

The game continues until all have competed. The team that finishes first wins. The same players may hold the clothes line throughout the game, but the game is more interesting if the exchange is made each time the towel is placed on the rope.

RUN AND TOSS RELAY

PLAYING FIELD: Gymnasium, playroom, or playground.

EQUIPMENT: Four beanbags or softballs to a team and chalk.

NUMBER OF PLAYERS: 20–40.

FORMATION: See diagram.

RULES OF THE GAME: Draw 4 circles for each team, one 10 feet from the starting line, then 2 circles 5 feet apart, and the fourth 10 feet farther. At a given signal, the first player takes the 4 beanbags or softballs to the first circle and tosses one of them back to the player at the front of the line. He then goes to the next circle and tosses the second object back to the player at the front of the line. He continues on to the next circle and then to the finish line. When he has thrown all 4 objects back, he returns to the rear of his team line, and next player continues the game. First team to finish wins.

SPOKE-CIRCLE CLUB-SNATCH RELAY

PLAYING FIELD: Gymnasium, playground, or playroom.

EQUIPMENT: Indian clubs or 3″ x 3″ wooden block.

NUMBER OF PLAYERS: 20–40.

FORMATION: See diagram.

RULES OF THE GAME: In the center of the circle, place one less Indian club or block than the number of teams playing. On a given signal, the last player of each team runs forward, attempting to retrieve a club. The player who does not obtain one is eliminated. The clubs are replaced, and the players receiving the clubs go to the head of their respective lines. On the signal, the second players run

SPOKE – CIRCLE   CLUB – SNATCH RELAY

out to secure a club. After all players have had a chance to run, the team with the most players wins. In the case of a tie between two teams, one club is placed in the middle circle, and the number one players attempt to rescue the club; the team securing the club is the winner. The second round begins with all players again in the game.

Scoring: 5 points each time a team wins.

PAIR RELAYS

BEANBAG HOBBLE-KICK RELAY

PLAYFIELD:	Gymnasium, playfield, or playroom.
EQUIPMENT:	Beanbags and inner tube rubber bands (one each for each team).
NUMBER OF PLAYERS:	12–40. Boys.
FORMATION:	See diagram.

RULES OF THE GAME: Place a beanbag and a rubber band at the head of each line. At a given signal, the first two players of each team place the rubber band over the ankles of their adjacent feet and kick the beanbag to the turn line and back. They then take the hobble off and give it to the next pair. The first team to get back to its original position wins the relay.

BEANBAG HOBBLE KICK RELAY

HOBBLES

DOUBLE HOBBLE RELAY

PLAYING FIELD: Gymnasium, playroom, or playground.

EQUIPMENT: None.

NUMBER OF PLAYERS: 20–40. Boys and girls.

FORMATION: See diagram.

RULES OF THE GAME: The players place the inside arm around each other's shoulders and grasp the ankle of the outside foot raised backward with the hand. At a given signal, the pair hops to the turning line and back, and sets off the next pair. While the first pair hops to the turning line and back, the second pair gets into position to start. If players lose their starting position while hopping, they must stop and resume this position before continuing the race. The team finishing first wins the relay.

DOUBLE HOBBLE RELAY

30' TO 80'

ELBOW PAIR RELAY

PLAYING FIELD: Gymnasium, playground, or play-
                        room.

EQUIPMENT: None.

NUMBER OF PLAYERS: 12–40. Boys and girls.

FORMATION: See diagram.

RULES OF THE GAME: The first two players of each team lock elbows. At a given signal, they run forward to the turning line and back to the starting line to set off the next pair. The first team to make two complete rounds wins the contest. If the elbows become unhooked, the pair must rehook them before continuing the relay.

FORWARD AND BACKWARD RELAY

PLAYING FIELD: Gymnasium, playroom, or play-
                        ground.

EQUIPMENT: None.

NUMBER OF PLAYERS: 20–40.

FORMATION: See diagram.

RULES OF THE GAME: One player faces forward and one backward; they link one elbow and walk to the turning line. They then walk to the starting line without turning around; thus, every

FORWARD AND BACKWARD RELAY

player walks both forward and backward. The team finishing first wins.

THREE-LEGGED RELAY

PLAYING FIELD: Gymnasium, playground, or playroom.

EQUIPMENT: Piece of rope, or inner tube 3" wide.

NUMBER OF PLAYERS: 12–40. Boys and girls.

FORMATION: See diagram.

RULES OF THE GAME: Tie the two inner legs together or slip a cut piece of inner tube over the feet to bind the legs of partners together. At a given signal, the first pair of each team runs to the turning line and back. When they have crossed the starting line, they take off the hobble and place it on the second pair. The first team to complete its round wins the relay.

TURN LINE **THREE-LEGGED RELAY**

SHUTTLE RELAYS

BOARD BALANCE FRONT AND BACK WALK

PLAYING FIELD: Gymnasium, playground, or playroom.

EQUIPMENT: Balance board, 10" x 6".

NUMBER OF PLAYERS: 12–40.

FORMATION: See diagram.

RULES OF THE GAME: At a given signal, the first players of teams on the "A" line walk to the "B" line with the balance board on their heads. As an "A" player crosses the "B" line, he hands the board to player number two, who walks backward to the "A" line. The

BOARD BALANCE FRONT AND BACK WALK

team that regains its original position first wins the contest. If the board falls from his head, a player must replace it before continuing.

BOTTLE AND STICK SHUTTLE RELAY

PLAYING FIELD:	Gymnasium, playground, playroom, or classroom.
EQUIPMENT:	Pop bottles and a 12″ stick or ruler.
NUMBER OF PLAYERS:	12–40.
FORMATION:	See diagram.

BOTTLE AND STICK SHUTTLE RELAY

RULES OF THE GAME: At a given signal, the first players at line "A" push the bottle with the stick to line "B." The player then hands the stick to the waiting number two player, who returns to line "A" pushing the bottle. The first team to regain its original position wins the contest. The same type and size of bottle should be used for all teams.

THE FARMER AND CROW SHUTTLE RELAY

PLAYING FIELD:	Gymnasium, playroom, or playground.

EQUIPMENT:	Four 6″ blocks of wood for each team; small stones also may be used.
NUMBER OF PLAYERS:	20–40. Boys.
FORMATION:	See diagram.

THE FARMER AND CROW SHUTTLE RELAY

RULES OF THE GAME: The Farmers start the relay. The first man of each team is given four small pieces of wood, and at a given signal, he places them on the floor at 5-foot intervals. When he crosses the starting line, the Crows hop on one foot and pick up the four pieces of wood and give them to the next Farmer in the opposite line, who in turn places them down.

Farmers become Crows, and Crows become Farmers, and the team that reaches its original position first wins the relay.

FORWARD-BACKWARD ROLL SHUTTLE RELAY

PLAYING FIELD:	Gymnasium.
EQUIPMENT:	Mats.
NUMBER OF PLAYERS:	12–24. Boys or girls.
FORMATION:	See diagram.

RULES OF THE GAME: At a given signal, the first player at line "A" runs to the mat, does *forward*-rolls to the end of the mat, and then runs to line "B" and touches off the number two player. The latter runs to the mat, does *backward*-rolls to the end of the mat, and touches off the number three player. The game continues until all players are back in their original positions. The first team to gain its original position wins the contest.

FORWARD-BACKWARD ROLL SHUTTLE RELAY

FROG AND CRAB SHUTTLE RELAY

PLAYING FIELD: Gymnasium, playroom, or playground.

EQUIPMENT: None.

NUMBER OF PLAYERS: 20–40. Boys or girls.

FORMATION: See diagram.

FROG AND CRAB SHUTTLE RELAY

CRABS   FROGS

RULES OF THE GAME: At a given signal, the Frogs spring forward in a squat position, lighting on the feet, balancing on the hands, and bringing the feet back under the body. The Frog continues to leap until he meets the Crab line; he then touches a Crab, who crawls back on all fours and touches off a Frog. The team getting back to its original position first wins the contest.

KANGAROO-HOP AND GOAT-BUTTING SHUTTLE RELAY

PLAYING FIELD: Gymnasium, playground, or play-room.

EQUIPMENT: Basketball, soccer ball, or volleyball.

NUMBER OF PLAYERS: 12–40.

FORMATION: See diagram.

B   ←— 30' TO 50' —→   A

RULES OF THE GAME: At a given signal, the first players at line "A" "kangaroo-hop" with the ball between their knees to line "B", where they give the ball to the number two players. The latter must "goat-butt" the ball on all fours with his head to line "A" to the number three players. The game continues until all players are back in their original positions. The first team to gain its original position wins the contest. If the ball is dropped from the knees, the player must recover the ball and return to the place where the ball was dropped before continuing. If the "Goat-Butter" loses control of his ball, he must recover it on all fours and butt it back to line "A."

Suggestion: If girls are not in gym suits, they should wear shorts when playing in mixed groups.

LOAD DOWN SHUTTLE RELAY

PLAYING FIELD: Playground, gymnasium, playroom, or classroom.

EQUIPMENT: An 8" rubber ball, basketball, soft-ball, volleyball, soccer ball, or bean-bag.

NUMBER OF PLAYERS: 12–40.

FORMATION: See diagram.

RULES OF THE GAME: At a given signal, the first players at line "A" pick up all four objects in the circle and run to the line "B" circle in which they place the objects. The first players at line "B" pick up the objects and run to the line "A," placing the objects in the "A" circle. The game continues until all players are back in their original positions; the first team to gain its original position wins the contest. If an object is dropped, the player must stop and recover it. For lower grades, use smaller objects.

B |← 20' TO 40' →| A

LOAD DOWN SHUTTLE RELAY

ROPE SKIP VARIATION RELAY

PLAYING FIELD: Gymnasium, playroom, or playground.

EQUIPMENT: A ⅜" skipping rope, 8' long.

NUMBER OF PLAYERS: 20–40.

FORMATION: See diagram.

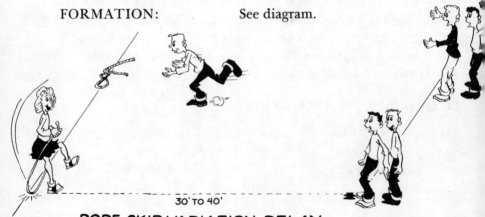

|← 30' TO 40' →|

ROPE SKIP VARIATION RELAY

RULES OF THE GAME: At a given signal, the first player of each team runs to the turning line, picks up the rope and jumps 3 times any style, places the rope back in position on the line, and returns to touch off the next player. The latter, however, must use a different style of jump. The game continues until all players have competed. The first team to finish wins.

Since each player on the team must use a different jump, every player must keep track of both teams' jumps. Such types of jumps as the following may be used:

Running, forward	Heel click
Running, backward	Hop on right foot
Cross arm, forward	Hop on left foot
Cross arm, backward	Hop swing left leg
Squat jump	Hop swing right leg
Rocking chair	Combinations of the above

SHUTTLE STEPPING STONES

PLAYING FIELD:	Gymnasium, playroom, or playground.
EQUIPMENT:	Pieces of cardboard or of paper carton, 8″ x 12″.
NUMBER OF PLAYERS:	20–40.
FORMATION:	See diagram.

RULES OF THE GAME: At a given signal, the first player places 2 pieces of cardboard on the floor, stepping on one and placing the other forward. He then steps on the forward piece, reaches back for the cardboard that is free, and places it ahead; he continues until he crosses the line. His teammate in the "B" section then uses the

12′ TO 20′

cardboard to walk back to the "A" line. The team finishing first wins. If a player misses the cardboard, he must go back and do it over.

LIMITED AREA RELAYS

BEANBAG BULL'S-EYE

PLAYING FIELD:	Gymnasium, playfield, playroom, or classroom.
EQUIPMENT:	Beanbag and chalk.
NUMBER OF PLAYERS:	12–40.
FORMATION:	See diagram.

RULES OF THE GAME: The first players of each team are given beanbags. At a given signal, they toss the beanbags at the first bull's eyes. If a beanbag falls within the bull's-eye without touching the circle line, the player picks it up, stands in the bull's-eye, and tosses at the next circle; he continues until he reaches the turning line. He then runs back to the starting line and gives the beanbag to the number two man. If the beanbag should fail to score a bull's-eye, the player must pick it up, go back to the last circle he has successfully made, and try again. The first team to complete its round wins.

Variation: Beanbag Bull's-Eye Shuttle Relay. Each team distributes its players equally at two lines. At a given signal, the first players at line "A" toss their beanbags at the first bull's-eyes. If a beanbag scores, the player picks it up, stands in the bull's-eye, and tosses at the next circle. When he reaches the "B" line, the first player there tosses the beanbag back toward the "A" line. The game continues until all players are back in their original positions. The first team to gain its original position wins the relay.

92

THE FREIGHT TRAIN

PLAYING FIELD: Gymnasium, playroom, or playground.

EQUIPMENT: None.

NUMBER OF PLAYERS: 20–40.

FORMATION: See diagram.

THE FREIGHT TRAIN

TURN LINE

RULES OF THE GAME: Divide the players into equal teams; the starting line will also be the finish line. Place the players at 10-foot intervals. At a given signal, the player at the end of each line runs to the next man in his line and clasps his hand upon the latter's hips. The two then run forward to the next player, and the leader clasps him on the hips. When the entire group has been connected, and has formed the train, the head man of the freight takes the train around the turning line and heads back to the finish line. If players break their clasp, the train must stop, and the front section of the train must reverse itself to pick up the others before they can continue to the finish line.

The first complete train passing over the finish line wins the relay.

20' TO 30'

TURN LINE

KICK THE BEANBAG

PLAYING AREA: Gymnasium, playroom, playground, or classroom.

EQUIPMENT: Beanbag for each team.

NUMBER OF PLAYERS: 20–40.

FORMATION: See diagram.

RULES OF THE GAME: Divide the group into equal teams. On a given signal, the number one player of each team kicks a beanbag to the turning line and back to the starting line. The next player in line proceeds in the same manner.

Variation: Shuttle beanbag kick relay.

30' TO 40'

SHUTTLE BEANBAG KICK RELAY

RING PASS RELAY

PLAYING FIELD: Classroom, playground, gymnasium, or playroom.

EQUIPMENT: Toothpicks and rings (washers or paperclips).

94

RING PASS RELAY

PASS

NUMBER OF PLAYERS: 12–30.

FORMATION: See diagram.

RULES OF THE GAME: Each player is given a toothpick and each team is given a ring. At a given signal, the first player of each team turns and passes the ring to the next player. No player may touch the ring unless it falls to the floor. If a player drops the ring, he must retrieve it, place it back on his toothpick, and again attempt to pass it. The game continues until the ring reaches the last player; he holds it on his toothpick and goes to the head of the line. The team whose last player reaches the head of the line first wins the contest.

Variation: Shuttle Ring Pass Relay. Players line up in shuttle teams. At a given signal, the number one player, toothpick in mouth, walks to the opposite line with the ring on his toothpick and gives it to the number two player. The latter goes back to the opposite line to give the ring to the number three player. The team that reaches its original position first wins.

|←————10' TO 20'————→|

SHUTTLE RING PASS RELAY

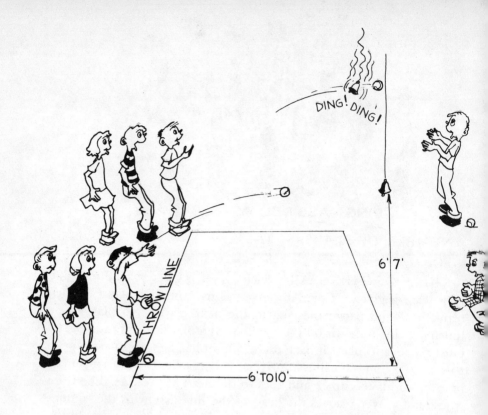

DING! DING!

THROW LINE

6' 7'

6' TO 10'

RING THE BELL RELAY

PLAYING FIELD: Classroom, gymnasium, or playroom.

EQUIPMENT: Small bells hanging on a string 6' or 7' from the floor and 2 tennis balls.

NUMBER OF PLAYERS: 12–30.

FORMATION: See diagram.

RULES OF THE GAME: Give each team a tennis ball. At a given signal, the number one player of each team tries to ring the bell by hitting it with the ball. Each player throws 5 times. The last player in the line acts as retriever; after the thrower has tossed his 5 balls, he takes the retriever's place. The team finishing first receives 3 points plus their bell rings. Each team receives 1 point for each bell ring. The players may take their time if they want to try for accuracy and not speed. All players must have a turn.

Variation: Give each team 50 throws at the bell. If a player misses, he retrieves the ball and throws back to the next player; if he hits the bell, he gets another throw. Have a scorekeeper for each team to keep count of the throws and hits.

SCHOOLROOM RELAY

PLAYING FIELD:	Classroom, gymnasium, playroom, or playground.
EQUIPMENT:	Dumbbell and a ruler for each team.
NUMBER OF PLAYERS:	10–40.
FORMATION:	See diagram.

SCHOOLROOM RELAY

RULES OF THE GAME: The first player of each team is given a ruler and a dumbbell. At a given signal, each starter, using the stick, rolls the dumbell up the left side of the aisle, down the right side, around the front desk or chairs, and then gives the stick to the next player in line, who continues the game. The first team to complete its round wins.

WOODEN LEG RELAY

PLAYING FIELD:	Classroom, gymnasium, playroom, or playground.
EQUIPMENT:	40″ broomstick.
NUMBER OF PLAYERS:	12–40.
FORMATION:	See diagram.

RULES OF THE GAME: The first player of each team is given a broomstick. The players curl either the right or left foot around the stick and hold the top with the hands. At a given signal, they hop on the "Wooden Leg" to the turning line and back to the starting line. They hand the stick to the next player, who proceeds in the same manner. The team finishing first wins the relay.

WOODEN LEG RELAY

Variation: Wooden Leg Shuttle Relay. At a given signal, the number one player of each team hobbles to the "B" line and gives the stick to the number two player; the latter heads for the "A" line. The game continues until players are back to their original positions. The first team to finish wins the contest.

WOODEN LEG SHUTTLE RELAY

ROPE SKIPPING

A. General information.
   1. Rope jumping is ideal for a modified program.
      a) It can be used any place at any time.
      b) It can be an individual activity or a group activity.
      c) The equipment cost is low.
      d) It can be as strenuous or as leisurely as desired.
      e) The program can be adjusted to meet individual needs, and the individual can progress at his own rate.
      f) It develops skill, rhythm, timing, and coordination; it develops right and left body parts equally, and gives good results when used to music.
   2. The rope should be ⅜″–½″ in diameter; a window sash cord can be used.
   3. The rope should be held between the thumb and index finger, the hands should be held out from the sides 12″ to 16″, and the upper arms should remain close to the body. The feet, ankles and knees should be kept together.
   4. Teach a system for rope skipping; instruct the learners to:
      a) Relax.
         (1) They should not be over-anxious and tense.
         (2) They should keep the head and eyes up, shoulders back, and chest out.
      b) Start out slowly.
         (1) They should try to jump as smoothly and gracefully as possible, landing on the balls of the feet with the knees slightly bent.
         (2) They should develop a sense of rhythm:
            (a) An increase or decrease in rhythm should be gradual, and jerky movements should be eliminated.
            (b) Jumps should be 1″ or 2″ off the floor.
      c) Rotate the hand in a 4″ or 5″ circle.
      d) Keep the rope going at a constant rhythm.

5. The activity may be carried on in a gymnasium, playroom, or playground.
6. These positions may be used in jumping rope.
   a) Forward and backward jump:
      Arms at the sides.
      Feet parallel.
      One end of rope in each hand.
      Knees straight.
      Elbows in.
   b) Crossed arm:
      Arms crossed at elbows.
      End of rope in each hand.
      Feet parallel.
   c) Squat jump:
      Knees together and pointing straight ahead.
      Trunk erect.
      Elbows close to body.
      End of rope in each hand.
   d) Double jump, one rope.
      Two face each other, feet together.
      Arms at the sides.
      Feet parallel.
      One person hold rope.
      Knees straight.
      Elbows in.
B. Individual rope jumping.
   1. Forward jump.
      Position: Forward jump.
      Action: Turn the rope forward with forearms and wrist, and jump on the toes.
   2. Backward jump.
      Position: Backward jump.
      Action: Turn the rope backward, and jump on the toes.

FORWARD JUMP

BACKWARD JUMP

POSITION   ACTION   POSITION   ACTION

1   2

RUNNING IN PLACE ~ FORWARD

3

RUNNING IN PLACE ~ BACKWARD

4

3. Running in place (forward).
    Position: Forward jump.
    Action: Turn the rope forward, and jump rope alternately, left foot, then right foot.

4. Running in place (backward).
    Position: Backward jump.
    Action: Turn the rope backward, and jump rope alternately, left foot, then right foot.

5. Running (forward).
    Position: Forward jump.
    Action: Run forward, progressing around the area, and turn the rope forward. Jump rope alternately, left foot, then right foot.

6. Running (backward).
    Position: Backward jump.
    Action: Run backward around the area, and turn the rope backward. Jump rope alternately, left foot, then right foot.

RUNNING FORWARD

5

RUNNING BACKWARD

6

C. Long rope doubles.
1. When introducing the long rope, have about 5 people in a group.
   a) Have 2 turners and 3 jumpers.
   b) Divide a large group by skills into players who cannot jump, who can stand still and jump, and who can run in and jump. The latter group can usually take care of itself by appointing a leader; the first and second groups need help to develop skills.
2. Use teaching aids for beginners.
   a) Swing the rope slowly back and forth in pendulum motion, allowing the jumpers to jump over the rope; this practice will aid the turners and the jumpers.
   b) Have the jumper stand in position while the rope is turned in a complete arc over his head. As the rope comes toward the jumper's feet, he should attempt to jump the rope. As the jumper builds up confidence, move on to the next step.
   c) Next, make a complete turn of the rope; have the jumpers attempt to run in and jump. While the rope is being turned, the jumper runs in, jumps, and runs out.
   d) As a jumper becomes more and more confident, he will enjoy chanting the many rope jumping rhymes.
3. Rope jumping.
   a) Running through the rope (forward).
      Position: Group stands on one side of the rope. Line should be at a 45 or 90 degree angle to the rope.
      Action: Turn the rope forward, run through under the rope and out without jumping.
   b) Running in, jumping, and running out (forward and backward).
      Action: Run in and jump once, then run out and line up on the opposite side to do the same action backward. Increase the number of jumps.
   c) High jumping.
      Action: Players try to jump the rope as it is gradually raised higher.

3. b   3. c

RHYTHMS

A. Rhythmical objectives.

Basic skills are necessary as a good foundation for rhythms. Fundamental rhythms include running, walking, skipping, hopping, and marching. It is assumed in this book that each child has been given an opportunity in the primary grades to experiment with these rhythms; however, if this is not the case, rhythms should begin with these basic skills, and the children should be taken from where they are in rhythm experience on to the dances found in this section. The fundamental rhythms necessary for enjoyment of dancing may be found in *Illustrated Games and Rhythms for Children—Primary Grades* by Frank H. Geri. Children should have the opportunity to take part in rhythm based on simple skills before they progress to the more complex dances. Opportunities should be offered for original compositions as well as for the familiar dances of far and near.

Everyone has rhythm. It is visible in all of nature and in all people. Dancing, like music and poetry, is one of the arts that live forever. Children are quick to respond to the stimulus of music, and although all are not born with the same rhythmic sense, all can develop an understanding, enjoyment, and awareness of the beauty of rhythm.

Boys and girls can dance together in elementary school. If the dance program of a school district has been a continuous process from kindergarten on, children accept it as a part of their regular activity. The usual problems encountered in the dance program, the shy boy, the timid girl, the "show-off," and the unskilled, are many times eliminated when dancing has been taught to boys and girls together throughout the grades.

The leader of a dance class has many satisfactions and many challenges. The instructor must be well prepared for the lesson and must be ready to meet the many demands of the children.

The rhythms in this book have been chosen carefully with the objectives of a good rhythm program in mind. They are designed to:

1. Develop a sense of rhythm.
2. Develop coordination and skill.
3. Develop the ability to express oneself through rhythm.
4. Develop poise and confidence.
5. Develop an awareness, understanding, and appreciation of rhythm.
6. Develop desirable social relationships through dance.
7. Develop understanding of people of other lands better through dance.

With these objectives in mind, couple, mixer, folk, singing, and square dances, contras, and play-party games have been included. The program should enrich and expand the experiences of the intermediate child and offer ample opportunity for each one to find a popular form of dance to enjoy.

Dance should offer many opportunities for listening. Let the music speak to the children and stimulate moods. It is important to consider the form of accompaniment to be used with the dance to fulfill the objectives of the program. It is important to have a piano or phonograph and records available for a successful program; however, in using a phonograph for the accompaniment, extreme care should be used in the selection of the recording. Record suggestions are made for each dance in this section, but the teacher should be very familiar with the record before attempting to use it. The instructor should be reminded that the tempo of a record is often unsatisfactory for the results desired, and by being familiar with the record before using it, the teacher may change the dance to fit the rhythm.

Tom-toms and drums are especially enjoyed by the children for they then have an opportunity to accompany as well as dance. For the basic skills and compositions, the percussion instruments are highly recommended. They are inexpensive to buy and oftentimes easily made by the children.

B. Techniques for rhythms.
1. Keep all directions clear and concise.
2. Let the children first enjoy the rhythm and then develop the skill.
3. Play the music so that they may become familiar with the musical

phrases, and then coordinate the activity with the music. Teach dances by phrases rather than by counting, so that a child may grasp an understanding of the music. Develop "good listeners."

4. Develop an understanding of specific terms, but do not talk down to the children. They will readily understand terms such as: single circle, promenade, counterclockwise, and clockwise.

5. Children learn more readily if they have an opportunity to observe that which they are expected to do. Use demonstrations.

6. When working with a large group, be sure everyone can hear. It is impossible for anyone to respond to directions unless he can hear clearly. Speak slowly and distinctly.

7. Be a part of the group when teaching a rhythm. Give your directions from the circle or line formation. Do not attempt to teach the entire dance before putting it to music. Let them learn a phrase, and then put it to music. After working out the entire dance, permit them to enjoy it before making suggestions for improvement.

8. Selection of partners should be varied in such a way as to guard against certain children always being chosen last. Partners should also be changed often within a period so that no one is "stuck" with the same partner.

   a) Line the boys up on one side of the room and the girls on the other. Lines may walk toward each other for partners, or they may turn and walk to the end of the room, meet, and come down the center in twos. This can be done to music.

   b) Counting-off methods may be used to get partners.

   c) Double circle, inside one of girls and the outside one of boys,

DOUBLE CIRCLE

PARTNERS FACING EACH OTHER

may be a variation used in getting a partner. The girls in the inside circle walk to their left while the boys in the outside circle walk to their right. On a given signal the circle stops, and the persons nearest each other are partners.

d) If there is an uneven number of children in the class, use the extra to assist with the accompaniment, or the teacher may dance after the instructions have been given. As soon as the dancers become proficient in the dance, the extra may "cut-in."

e) When there are more girls than boys in the class, have some girls dance together; if there are more boys, have some boys dance together. This procedure creates no problem if it is used regularly.

C. Folk and square dance terminology.

1. Allemande left: the boy takes the left hand of the corner girl in his left hand, and walks around her as she walks around him. Each comes back to his original position. A forearm hold may be be used.

2. Allemande right: the boy takes his partner's right hand in his right hand (unless the call directs otherwise), and walks around her as she walks around him. Each comes back to his original position. A forearm hold may be used.

3. Balance: all join hands, the boy's right with the girl's left, and step back one step and do a slight curtsy. All then join inside hands, face partners, step back one step, and do a slight curtsy. (This form of the balance is often used at the beginning of the square dance when followed by a swing.)

4. Circle: all join hands, the boys' palms upward, and move to the left or right as directed by the caller.

PARTNERS FACING INWARD

SINGLE CIRCLE   PARTNERS FACING INWARD

SINGLE CIRCLE   PARTNERS FACING

CLOCKWISE   COUNTERCLOCKWISE

PLAIN QUADRILLE FORMATION

PARTNERS SIDE-BY-SIDE

PARTNERS FACING

DOUBLE-LINE FORMATION

5. Corner: the person on each dancer's left.
6. Do-pas-O: it is called for a circle of 4, 6, or 8. The boy takes his partner's left hand in his left hand and walks around her; he then reaches for his corner's right hand with his right hand and walks around her. He goes back to his partner with his left hand, places his right at her waist, and walks her forward as they turn to complete the figure.
7. Dos-sa-dos: the two dancers face each other, walk forward passing

right shoulders, slide across behind each other, and move back to their original positions without turning.

8. Forearm hold: the open palm is placed against the partner's forearm, the elbows are bent, the forearms held horizontal: there is no grip.

9. Forward and back: all walk forward three steps (unless otherwise directed), balance, and walk back three steps.

10. Grand right and left: all partners face each other, join right hands, pass each other by and give the left hand to the next advancing person, the right to the next, left to the next, etc. Partners meet across the square from their original position.

11. Honor: all dancers bow or curtsy to their partners or corners, as the call directs.

BOW   CURTSY

HONOR   SKATERS' OR PROMENADE   FOREARM HOLD

12. Ladies chain:

a) In the two ladies chain, the two girls step forward, clasp right hands, pass each other, and extend their left hands to the opposite boys. The latter turn the girls forward with their right hands behind their waists. The two ladies meet with their right hands again, and extend their left hands to their own partners, who turn them forward to their original positions.

b) In the Grand chain, or four ladies chain, the four girls right-hand-star to the opposite boys, who turn them forward with their left hands. The girls then star back to their own partners, who turn them forward with their left hands with right hands at their waists.

LADIES CHAIN

RIGHT AND LEFT THROUGH

13. Line of direction: the circular movement is counterclockwise, unless otherwise directed.

14. Partner: the boy and girl dancing together are partners; the girl on the boy's right, and the boy on the girl's left are partners.

15. Pass through: the two couples facing each other walk forward. The girls pass between the opposite couple, while boys walk around the outside. They do not turn around, but wait for the next call.

16. Promenade:

    a) In the skater's position, the girl walks on the right, the boy on the left; they join hands right to right, and left to left, with their right hands on top.

    b) In the Single file, the girl walks in front of the boy.

    c) In the Varsouvianna, the girl is on the right, with the boy's right hand crossed behind her shoulder to hold her right hand. The girl's arm is bent at elbow, and her right hand is held outside and in front of her right shoulder. The boy's left hand holds her's in front of his left shoulder.

17. Right and left through: two couples facing each other walk forward. The girls pass between the opposite couple, and the boys walk on the outside. The boy takes his partner's left hand, places his right hand around her waist, and turns her forward and

RIGHT AND LEFT BACK

around after they have passed by the opposite couple. The girl moves forward on the turn, and her right hand, palm out, is on her right hip.

Variation: As the couples walk forward, they touch right hands with the opposite couple in passing through. This movement may be used as a teaching device, also.

18. Sashay: the couple moves to the side with a slide-close-slide hold movement. In the open position, the boy moves three steps across behind the girl, while she moves three steps across in front of him. They have changed places, and the girl is now on her partner's left. The next call could be a re-sashay, which would place them back in their original positions.

19. Swing: this movement is frequently indicated specifically by the caller.

RIGHT ELBOW SWING   LEFT ELBOW SWING

CROSS ARMS

TWO-HAND SWING   TWO-HAND SWING
        I   II

   a) In the buzz swing, the dancers assume the social dance position, but with right hips side by side. The outside of the partners' right feet should be touching; the left foot is placed

111

about six inches to the side. The partners lean away from each other, make quick light steps on the balls of the right feet, and push themselves around with the left feet.

b) In the walk swing, the dancers assume the social dance position with right hips side by side. The partners lean away from each other and swing with quick, light walk-steps.

c) In the two-hand swing, the partners join both hands, pull away from each other, and swing. A quick, running or buzz step is used.

d) In the elbow swing, the boy meets his partner with his right arm bent at the elbow. They hook right arms, pull back away from each other, and buzz-step swing.

e) In the forearm swing, the boy meets his partner and places his right forearm against hers. With elbows straight and forearms horizontal, they pull away from each other and swing with a quick running step.

D. Social dance positions.

1. Closed position: the girl's right hand rests in boy's left, the boy's right hand is held on his partner's shoulder blade, and the girl's left hand lies on the boy's shoulder. Partners face each other.

SOCIAL DANCE   SEMI-OPEN   OPEN

2. Semi-open position: the partners face in the line of direction. The girl's right hand rests in the boy's left, the boy's right hand is held on his partner's shoulder blade, and the girl's left hand lies on the boy's shoulder.

3. Open position: the boy has his partner on his right; their inside hands are joined. The girl's right hand is on her skirt, the boy's left hand is tucked, palm out, behind his waist, and both face in the line of direction.

VARSOUVIANNA   FACE-TO-FACE AND BACK-TO-BACK POLKA

4. Varsouvianna position: the dancers stand side by side, with the girl on the boy's right. His right hand crosses behind her shoulder to hold her right hand. The girl's right hand, arm bent at elbow, is held outside and in front of her right shoulder. His left hand holds hers in front of his left shoulder.

5. Banjo or side-by-side position: the partners assume social dance position, and step side by side, right sides together.

6. Face-to-face and back-to-back polka position: the partners join inside hands (boy's right and girl's left), and turn and face each other. Moving to the boy's left and to the girl's right with a polka step, on the hop, partners turn so that they stand back-to-back. The hands remain joined.

THE ACE OF DIAMONDS—*Danish*—*R.C.A. Victor 20989, 45-6169;* *Methodist 102*

Formation:
    Double circle, boys on the inside, partners facing each other.

Directions:

1. Clap hands.
2. Hook right elbows and swing to the left with 3 running steps.
3. Clap hands.
4. Hook left elbows and swing to the right with 3 running steps.
5. Repeat 1–4.
6. Arms folded, partners dance 4 step-hops toward the center, boy backs up and girl moves forward.
7. Four step-hops back to place, girl backs up and boy moves forward.
8. Place hands on partner's shoulders, and with 4 step-hops circle once to the right.
9. Open position, inside hands joined, polka face-to-face and back-to-back.

POLKA

BADGER GAVOTTE—*American—Decca 24147, 25062; Linden 135*

Formation:

Couples, open position, inside hands joined.

Directions:

1. Walk forward 4 steps.
2. Partners face, join both hands and slide 3 steps to the boy's left. On the fourth count, the boy points his right toe to his right, the girl points her left toe to her left.
3. Repeat 1 and 2 in the reverse line of direction, pointing to the boy's left and the girl's right.
4. Do 8 slow two-steps in dance position.

2.

1.

3.

4.

BADGER GAVOTTE

Variation:

The two-step may be done in open position with a face-to-face and back-to-back movement.

BLEKING —*Swedish*—*R.C.A. Victor 45-6169*

Formation:

Single circle, partners facing, both hands joined.

Directions:

LEFT HOP — HOP

1. Bleking step.
   a) Hop on left foot. Bring right heel and right arm forward, elbow straight. Right hand in front of partner's shoulder. Left arm comes well back with elbow bent.
   b) Repeat with the hop on the right foot. The *a* and *b* of the Bleking Step are slow.
2. In quick succession, repeat the hops of the Bleking Step 3 times.
3. Turn.

RIGHT HOP — HOP

   a) Join hands shoulder high. Use a windmill movement of the extended arms.
   b) Both hop twice on each foot, at the same time swinging the arms up and down. Boy's right arm is down when hopping on right foot, and left arm is down when hopping on the left foot.
   c) Turn when hopping.
4. Repeat the dance.

STEP-HOP

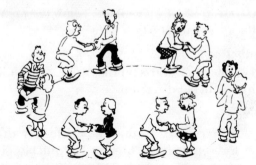

BLEKING SWEDISH FOLK DANCE

115

Formation:

The Bleking Step is necessary in the instruction of some folk dances. It may be taught in a line formation with the students facing the instructor, or it may be taught in the single circle such as is used in the folk dance, Bleking.

1.

Directions:

Position: Partners face, both hands joined.

1. Hop on the right foot and bring the left leg forward in an extended position with the left heel on the floor, toe up. At the same time, extend the left arm forward at shoulder height. Bend the right arm at the elbow.

2. Repeat step 1, hopping on the left foot and bringing the right leg forward in an extended position with the right heel on the floor, toe up. At the same time, extend the right arm forward, shoulder high, and bend the left arm at the elbow.

2.

3. Repeat the above steps at double time, 3 times.

R,L,R
L,R,L
R,L,R

During the quick footwork, the arms are alternately extended.

BROOM DANCE—*The Waltz You Saved for Me, Imperial 1182; Whisper Waltz, Victor 21-0489*

Formation:

Double circle, boys on the inside, all inside hands joined, all facing in the line of direction.

Directions:

1. Players walk around the circle to waltz rhythm. One player in the center has a broom. He quickly gives it to someone in the circle and takes his place. The one who receives the broom moves quickly about the circle and hands someone else the

BROOM DANCE

broom. The one who has the broom at the end of the music sits out a dance. Couples waltz around the room until a given signal (whistle or music stops). At the signal, they dance into a double circle and the broom is again passed around the circle.

CAPTAIN JINKS—*R.C.A. Victor Album c-36; Decca 18222; Methodist 103*

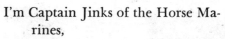

I'm Captain Jinks of the Horse Ma-
rines,
I feed my horse good corn and
beans,
I swing the ladies in their teens, for
that's the style in the army!

I teach the ladies how to dance,
How to dance, how to dance,
I teach the ladies how to dance, for
that's the style in the army!

Salute your partner, turn to the
right,
And swing your neighbor with all
your might,
Then promenade with the lady
right, for that's the style in the
army!

117

FACE PARTNER

PROMENADE

SALUTE

CHANGE PARTNERS

Directions:

1. March forward in the line of direction. On the word "beans," the girls turn, face partners, and join hands.
2. Both skip, with hands joined in small circle.
3. In promenade position, skip forward around the circle.
4. On the words "Salute your partner," partners face and salute with the right hand.
5. The boys turn to the girl behind, their corner girl, and swing her once around.
6. Promenade with new partner.

COTTON-EYED JOE—*Imperial 1045; Folkraft 1035*

1.a.

1.b.

2.a.   2.b.

Formation:

Couples with both hands joined; boys have backs to center of floor.

Directions:

1. The boy begins with his left foot and the girl with her right; they do a heel and toe movement 3 steps to the left side: left, right, left, for the boy, and right, left, right, for the girl.
2. Repeat 1 with the opposite footwork. Cue calls for Steps 1 and 2 might be:
   a) Left heel and toe, step, together, step.
   b) Right heel and toe, step, together, step.

3.

4.

3. Each makes a complete turn, the boy to his left, the girl to her right. While making the turn, each takes 12 small, stamp steps or 4 polka steps.

4. Partners, face to face, take 4 push steps away from each other and 4 back. The push step is done by the boy placing his weight on his left foot and pushing away with his right, while the girl places her weight on her right foot and pushes away with her left. They thus move in the same direction.

5. In promenade position, couples move in the line of direction around the room with 4 two-steps.

Repeat the entire dance as many times as desired.

5.

THE CRESTED HEN—*Danish*—*R.C.A. Victor 45-6176, 21619;*
Methodist 108

1.

2.

Formation:

Groups of three, 1 boy and 2 girls.

Directions:

1. Dancers join hands and skip to the left 8 steps.

2. Stamp and skip 8 steps to the right.

3. Boys and girls continue to hold hands; they then release hand and place it at waist. The right hand girl skips through an arch formed by the boy and the left hand girl; the boy follows her and turns under his own arm. The left hand girl

119

then follows and goes under the arch formed by the boy and right hand girl; the boy follows her and turns under his own arm.

4. The dance is repeated.

3.a:

b.

c.

d.

CSEBOGAR –*Hungarian*–*R.C.A. Victor 20992, 45-6182*

Formation:

Single circle, hands joined, facing center.

Directions:

1. Join hands, take 7 slide steps to the left.
2. Pause on eighth count.
3. Take 7 slide steps to the right.
4. Pause.
5. Skip 4 steps to the center of the circle.
6. Skip backward 4 steps.
7. Turn; partners hook right elbows, and, with left arm held high above the head, skip 4 steps to the left.
8. Partners face each other forming a single circle: boys face counter-clockwise, girls face clockwise. Join both hands and take 4 slow slides toward the center of the circle.
9. Four slow slides back to place.
10. Two slides toward the center.

1.

2.

3.

4.

5.

6.

7.

11. Two slides back to place.
12. Repeat the turn, ending the dance with a shout.

HEY!

DOWN SOUTH MIXER—*American*—*Decca 25067; Windsor 7122*

Formation:

Double circle, facing in the line of direction, inside hands joined, boys on the inside.

Directions:

1. Walk 4 steps forward, beginning with the outside foot.

2. Continuing in the line of direction, face partner, join both hands, and slide 4 steps.
3. Face reverse line of direction in open position, inside hands joined, and walk 4 steps.
4. Continuing in the reverse line of direction, slide 4 steps with both hands joined.

5.

6.

5. Partners facing, both hands joined, do 4 step-points. The boy steps his left foot to the side and touches it behind the heel with the toe of his right foot. The girl steps her right foot to the side and touches it behind the heel with the toe of her left foot. On the next step-point, the boy steps right and the girl left.

6. Partners dos-a-dos: the two dancers move around each other passing right shoulder to right shoulder and back to back, and return to the original position.

7. Every boy and girl moves one person to his left, and all have new partners to begin the dance again.

8. The entire dance may be repeated as often as desired.

9. Cue Calls:
   a) Walk 2, 3, 4.
   b) Slide 2, 3, 4.
   c) Walk 2, 3, 4; Slide 2, 3, 4.
   d) Four step-points.
   e) Dos-a-Dos and get a new partner.

DOWN THE CENTER AND DIVIDE THE RING—*American—*
Capitol BD44

Formation:
   Square.

Directions and calls:
   1. "Honor your partner."
      Boy bows to partner; girl curtsies.
   2. "Honor your corners too."
      Boy bows to the left hand girl; girl curtsies.
   3. "Now allemande left, that's what you do." **1.**
      Every boy turns to his corner girl, extends his left hand to her, and shakes hands the wrong way. They walk all the way around each other, until the boy is back facing his own partner.
   4. "It's a right to your partner, grand right and left."
      The boys extend right hands to their own partners, pass her by, and give the coming girl a left hand; this continues until each

2.   3.   4.

boy meets his own partner across the square from his home place.

5. "Now promenade two by two, as you always do."

5.

6.   7.

Partners meet, join hands in skaters position, and walk in the line of direction to home place in the square.

6. "Head couple balance and swing."

Couple #1, inside hands joined, turn and face each other, raise joined hands, take one step backward, then step together and swing.

7. "Down the center and divide the ring; the girl goes Gee and the boy goes Haw. Swing when you meet; swing at the head and swing at the feet."

The first couple walks down the center of the set, splits the third couple apart, and the girl turns to her right and walks around the outside of the square to home. The boy turns to his left and walks around the outside of the square to meet his partner at home. The first and third couples swing.

8. "Down the center as you did before, down the center and cut away four. Swing when you meet; swing at the head and swing at the feet."

The first couple walks down the center of the set as in Figure 7. As they face the third couple, they separate, and the boy walks between girl number three and boy number four; the girl walks between boy number three and girl number two.

They walk around the outside of the square and meet at home. The first and second couples swing.

9. "Down the center as you always do, down the center and cut away two. Everybody swingeroo."

The first couple walks to the middle of the set, the boy turns to his left and walks between the fourth couple, and the girl turns to her right and walks between the second couple. They return home, and everybody swings.

10. "Now allemande left with your left hand."

Each boy turns toward his corner, extends his left hand, and walks all the way round with hands clasped until facing his own partner.

11. "A right to your partner, grand right and left. You meet old Sal, you meet old Sue, you meet your gal and promenade, that's what you do."

Boys extend their right hands to their partners, pass by, give the next the left hands, and continue until they meet their partners across the square from the home place. Join hands, skaters position, and walk home.

The dance continues for the second, third, and fourth couples. Variations may be made in the opening and the allemande trims.

GLOW WORM MIXER—*Imperial 1044; Old Timer 8004; MacGregor 310; Windsor 7613*

> *Formation:*
> Double circle, facing counterclockwise, inside hands joined, boys on the inside.

Directions:

1. Walk or skip 4 steps forward in the line of direction.
2. Face partner and back away from each other 4 steps. Boys back toward center of the circle and girls toward the outside.
3. Everyone look one person to the right of partner, and walk or skip 4 steps toward this new partner.
4. Join right elbows and walk or skip 4 steps around to the right. The girl then makes a slight turn to form the double circle with her new partner.
5. Begin the dance again.
6. Cue calls:
   a) Walk 2, 3, 4.
   b) Back 2, 3, 4.
   c) Together 2, 3, 4.
   d) Around 2, 3, 4.

GUSTAF'S SKOAL—*Swedish Folk Dance—R.C.A. Victor 20988A, 45-6170; Methodist 108*

Formation: Quadrille

Directions: Gustaf's Skoal is a Swedish dance which shows both the dignity and love for fun of the Swedish people. *Skoal* means "a toast."

1. Measure 1-2: head couples, the first and third, walk 3 slow steps forward, and bow to opposite couple.
2. Measure 3-4: head couples walk 4 slow steps back to place.

125

3. Measure 5-8: side couples, the second and fourth, repeat action of head couples.

4. Measure 9-12: side couples grasp inside hands and form arch with hands held high. Head couples skip to center of set, make a quarter turn to face corner side couple, join hands with original opposites, skip through arch, separate, and skip to home place.

5. Measure 13-16: Everyone clap hands once, join both hands with partner, and skip in place turning to the right. Pull away from each other for one complete swing.

6. Measure 9-16: Repeat with the head couples forming the arch, and the side couples skipping around and back to place.

7. Cue calls:

   a) Walk 1, 2, 3; bow.

   b) Back 2, 3, 4.

   c) Repeat the calls for sides.

   d) Skip 2, 3.

   e) Clap; swing 2, 3, 4.

HANSEL AND GRETEL—*R.C.A. Victor 45-6182*

Formation:

Double circle, partners facing each other, boys on the inside.

Directions:

1. Boys bow; girls curtsy.
2. Partners join right hands and left hands.
3. Boys point left toe forward in the line of direction and return to place.
4. Hands joined, everyone takes 4 slides to the gents' left.
5. Repeat steps 3 and 4, going in the reverse direction with opposite toe movement.
6. Everyone faces in the line of direction with hands crossed in skaters position, and promenades forward 8 steps and then skips forward 8 steps.
7. Partners turn and face each other again, boy on the inside; they hesitate, then tap left foot and right foot, hesitate, and clap hands 3 times.
8. Repeat actions 3 through 5.
9. Repeat 5 through 7, and have dancers nod the head 3 times and snap the fingers 3 times, instead of tapping and clapping.
10. Repeat 3 through 5.

1.

2.

3.

4.

5.

6.

HEEL AND TOE POLKA—*MacGregor 400*

Formation:

Same as Couple Polka.

Directions:

See the two-step.

1. Touch the left heel forward, toes up, and lean backward.

1.

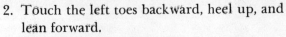

2. Touch the left toes backward, heel up, and lean forward.
3. Two-step left: the third step of the Heel and Toe Polka may be changed to suit the age level. Small children may use 3 running steps instead of the polka two-step.
4. Repeat for the right foot.

Variation: The heel-toe two-step movement may be followed by 16 two-steps or polka steps.

IRISH WASHERWOMAN MIXER—*R.C.A. Victor 45-6178; Imperial 1039; Folkraft 1044; Methodist 103*

Formation:
Single circle, hands joined, boys and girls alternated.

Directions:
1. Everyone walks 4 steps into the center.
2. Walk 4 steps backward to place.
3. Tap right foot 4 times in place.

1.

2.

3.

4. Swing the left hand girl (the corner) twice around. Join right elbows for the swing and skip twice around to the right.

5. A double circle is formed, with everyone facing counterclockwise, boys on the inside and girls on the outside. The boy swings the girl who was his partner in step 4, and they join hands and promenade forward 16 steps in the line of direction.

6. Repeat the dance from the beginning.

7. Cue calls:
   a) Walk 2, 3, 4.
   b) Back 2, 3, 4.
   c) Tap 2, 3, 4.
   d) Swing corner round and round.
   e) Promenade new partner.

4.

5.

Formation:

Double circle, boys on the inside, with hands joined.

Directions:

1. Eight face-to-face and back-to-back polka steps.
2. Four heel-toe polka steps.
3. Face partner: bow and clap hands 3 times.
4. Repeat Step 3.
5. Clap partner's right hand, own hand, partner's left hand and own hand.
6. Both make a complete turn to the left.
7. Shake right forefinger, then left forefinger. Join both hands and make a complete turn to the boy's left.
8. Repeat Steps 3-7.
9. Dancers move to the left and secure a new partner. The entire dance may be repeated as often as desired.

130

LA RASPA—*Mexican Social Dance—Methodist 106; Folkraft 1119;*
Victor 20,3189

1.

2.

3.

4.

Formation:

Double circle, partners facing, both hands joined; boys on the inside circle. Directions are for the boys; girls do the counterpart.

Directions:

1. Hop on the left foot and extend the right foot forward, heel down.
2. Hop on the right foot and extend the left foot forward, heel down.
3. Hop quickly 3 times, alternating the extension of the heel.
4. Repeat 1, 2, 3 for a total of 4 Bleking type steps.
5. Hook right elbows and run around each other 8 counts; clap.
6. Hook left elbows and run around each other 8 counts; clap.
7. Repeat 5 and 6.
8. Begin dance again.
9. Cue calls:
   a) Right—left.
      Right, left, right.
         or
   b) Hop—Hop.
      Hop, hop, hop.
      Run.

5.

131

LILLI MARLENE—*Mixer or Couple Dance—Folkraft 1096;*
MacGregor 310

Formation:

Double circle facing counterclockwise, boys on the inside, hands joined, and girls on the outside.

1.

Directions:

1. Walk forward in the line of direction 4 walking steps.
2. Face partner and slide on in the same direction 3 steps. Hold the fourth count.
3. Face clockwise and walk forward in the reverse line of the original direction 4 steps.
4. Slide 4 steps in the reverse line of direction.

2.

3.

4.

5.

5. Facing partner, do 4 step swings. The boy steps on his left foot and swings his right leg across in front of his body, steps on the right foot, and swings his left leg across in front of his body. He repeats this movement. The girl does the same movement, but begins with a right step, so that the swing movement is in the same direction for both the boy and girl.

6. Facing counterclockwise around the room once again, couples walk forward 3 steps, turn toward partners, walk 3 steps in the reverse line of direction, and turn again at the end of the 3 steps to face counterclockwise. Each time a turn is made, quickly change hands so that inside hands are joined.

6.

7. Facing counterclockwise around the room, partners do 4 face-to-face and back-to-back two-steps or polka steps in the line of direction, and the boy then does 4 two-steps in a small circle to his left and back to his partner, while she two-steps to her right and back around.

8. Cue calls:
   a) Walk 2, 3, 4.
      Slide and slide and slide.
   b) Repeat the above.
   c) Step swing, step swing, step swing.
      Walk three.
      Two-step.

7.

Variation: If the dance is done as a mixer, on step 7 the girls two-step on the last 4 two-steps to the boy behind, and thus everyone gets a new partner.

133

LITTLE MAN IN A FIX—*Danish—R.C.A. Victor 20449; Linden 703; Folk Dance Record 1054*

Formation:

Groups of 4. Boys place their right arms around their partners' waists, and the boys of two couples join left elbows. The girls put their right hands on their hips and their left hands on their partners' shoulders. Thus, one couple faces clockwise and the other counter-clockwise.

Directions:

1.

1. Run forward 16 steps with knees held high.
2. Without hesitation, the boys join left hands, form an arch, and take their partners by their left hands; the girls run in front of their partners under the arch, turn and face each other, and join hands. Pulling backward, they run to the right 16 steps.
3. Partners face each other, the boy places his hands on the girl's waist, she places her hands on his shoulders, and they waltz. If the waltz step has not been given to the group, they may merely walk to waltz rhythm.
4. Every couple finds a new couple to dance with. If there was an odd couple, they try to get into the dance at this time.

2.

Variations:

3.

1. A face-to-face, back-to-back waltz may be used in Step 3. This is done by having the boy take his partner's left hand in his right and begin with his left foot, while the girl begins with her right; they waltz, turning away from each other, and then repeat the waltz step facing each other.
2. The boy may take his partner's left hand in his right in Step 3 and walk to waltz tempo.

134

NORWEGIAN MOUNTAIN MARCH—*R.C.A. Victor 20151, 45-6173;*
Folk Dance Record Album B, 345-346

1.

2.

3.

Formation:

Groups of 3, move counterclockwise around the room. Number one stands in front of Numbers two and three, who join inside hands. Number two joins left hands with Number one, and Number three joins right hands with Number one.

Directions:

The step used throughout the dance is a running step of 3 counts with emphasis on the first count.

1. Beginning with the left foot, all run around the room in the line of direction 16 measures. Emphasize the first count by bending the body slightly to the left and to the right.

2. Number one dances backward under the joined hands of two and three, while two and three dance in place; two measures.

3. Number two dances in front of Number one and turns inward under Number one's right arm; two measures.

4. Number three turns inward under Number one's right arm; two measures.

5. Number one turns to the right under his own right arm; all now should be back in the original formation. While dancing 2-5, everyone should dance the rhythm in place. While dancing 1, the leader should look over his left and right shoulder as if to see that his partners are coming with him.

4.

5.

OH, JOHNNY—*Imperial 1099; Folkraft F1037; Old Timer 8043; MacGregor 646*

Formation:

Single circle, dancers facing the center, hands joined, boys and girls alternating around the circle.

Directions and Calls:

1. "Oh, you all join your hands and circle the ring." Everyone joins hands and circles to the left.

2. "Stop where you are and give your partner a swing." Everyone stops, the boy turns to the girl at his right, they join both hands and make one complete turn to the left.

3. "Then you swing the one behind you." The boys all turn and swing their corner girl.

4. "Then you swing your own, that is, if you have time to." The boy returns to his own partner and swings her again.

5. "Then you allemande left with the sweet corner maid." The boy turns and faces his left-hand girl again. They join left hands as though doing a wrong-way handshake. They walk all the way round each other with left hands joined, and stop when they are facing their original partners again.

6. "Dos-A-Dos your own." The boy and his partner walk all the way around each other, passing right shoulder to shoulder, back to back, and return to place.

7. "Then you all promenade with the sweet corner maid, singing 'Oh, Johnny, Oh, Johnny, Oh!'" The boy turns and takes his corner maid in a crossed-arm position, the skaters' position, and promenades counterclockwise around the room.

1.

2.

3.

4.

5.   6.   7.

Formation:

Single circle, all face center, girls and boys alternating.

Directions:

1. Girls skip 4 skips into the circle, then skip backward to place.
2. Boys skip 4 skips into the circle, then skip backward to place.
3. Repeat 1 and 2; This portion of the dance takes the verse of the music thru twice.
4. Chorus: Boys face their partners and do a grand right and left, which continues once through the chorus. When the chorus repeats, each boy takes the girl coming toward him in promenade position, and with this new partner, skips or walks counterclockwise around the circle.

Formation:

Single circle, hands joined, with boys and girls alternating; odd man (Dan Tucker) in the center.

Directions and Calls:

1. "Balance one and balance all." With hands joined, all step toward Dan Tucker, raise hands, and step back into place.

2. "Turn to the left, for a left allemande." The boy turns to his corner girl and gives her his left hand and they walk all the way around.

3. "And a right to your partner all around the hall." From the left allemande, boys face their own partners and extend their right hands to them and they walk all the way around.

4. "Grand right and left, and you meet Old Sue and you meet Old Saul." Boys pull by their partners with their right hands and meet the girls coming with the left; they pull by them and meet the next with the right. During the grand right and left, Dan Tucker joins the circle. The grand right and left is continued until the leader calls the next figure.

5. "Promenade one and promenade all." When the leader calls promenade, each boy gets the girl coming toward him for a partner, and, with hands crossed in skaters' position,

138

they walk counterclockwise, boys on the inside, around the hall. The man left out becomes the next Dan Tucker.

6. "Join your hands, and into the center, and back right out." Everyone joins hands in a single circle and walks 4 steps toward the center and 4 steps back to place.

7. "Circle to the left." With hands joined, all move to the left in the grand circle.

8. Begin the dance again.

9. The dance may be brought to a finish with a "Swing your partner and promenade right off the floor."

POLKA—*2/4 Time—Any good polka record may be used; Victor 26-1013 (Emila Polka); MacGregor 653*

Formation:

The two-step may be taught in a line formation with the students facing the instructor or in a circle formation with all hands joined.

Directions:

Directions are given for the boys; the girls do the counterpart, beginning with the opposite foot. Position: Social dance or open.

1. The polka step is the two-step, with the addition of a hop before the first step. Hop right and step forward on the left foot.
2. Bring the right foot to the left foot, and transfer weight to the right foot.
3. Step forward again on left foot.

POP GOES THE WEASEL—*American Contra—R.C.A. Victor 20151,*
45-6180; Folkraft Album F2; Methodist 104; MacGregor A1.4

Formation:
Double line, 6 couples in a set.

Directions and Calls:

1. "Head couple down center and back to place."
   The head couple join hands, slide to the end of the set, and slide back to the head of the line.

2. "Head couple cast off."
   The head boy skips down the outside of his line, while each boy turns and follows in line; the girl skips down the outside of her line, while each girl follows. The head couple leads the lines back to place.

3. "Head couple balance with the second in line."
   The head couple joins hands with the second girl, and the three step back, raising their hands slightly.

4. "Circle three and around you go."
   Head couple circles with the second girl once and a half; this places them in a position to face the second boy.

5. "Pop under you go and on to the next."
   The head couple raise their arms, pull the second girl under the arch formed, and then move over to the second boy. Steps 4 and 5 are repeated with a zig-zagging movement until all have been "popped under."

6. "Head couple up center to cast off."

6.

Repeat the cast off movement after the head couple has returned to the head of the set. This time, the cast off gets a new head couple: the former head couple forms an arch at the end of the set, and the others join hands as they go under the arch to their positions in the set. The second couple thus is placed at the head of the set, while the first head couple is now its foot.

7. The dance is repeated until all couples have been at the head of the set.

POP GOES THE WEASEL—*Victor 20151, 45-6180; Folkraft Album F2; Methodist 104; MacGregor A1. 4*

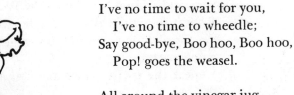

'Round and 'round the cobbler's bench,
 The monkey chased the weasel,
In and out, and 'round about;
 Pop! goes the weasel.

Penny for a spool of thread,
 Penny for a needle;
That's the way the money goes,
 Pop! goes the weasel.

I've no time to wait for you,
 I've no time to wheedle;
Say good-bye, Boo hoo, Boo hoo,
 Pop! goes the weasel.

All around the vinegar jug,
 The monkey chased the weasel;
The monkey pulled the stopper out;
 Pop! goes the weasel.

Formation:

Double circle, inside hands joined, boys facing in the line of direction on the inside.

Directions:

1. Starting with the outside foot, walk forward 3 steps and point the inside foot forward.
2. Repeat Step 1, starting with the inside foot and pointing the outside foot after 3 steps.
3. Partners face. Boy steps to the side with the left foot and swings the right foot forward as he bends both knees. The girl steps to the side with the right foot and swings the left foot forward as she bends both knees.
4. Repeat Step 3 in the opposite direction.
5. With the boy's right hand and the girl's left joined, the girl skips under the boy's right arm, and all sing "Pop! goes the Weasel."
6. Repeat the entire dance; the boy skips under the girl's left arm and moves back to get a new partner.
7. Repeat the entire dance as many times as desired.

RIGHT-HAND LADY WITH THE RIGHT-HAND GENT
—American—Capitol Album BD44

Formation:
  Quadrille.

Directions and Calls:
  1. "Honor your partner."
    Boy bows and girl curtsies.
  2. "And your corners all."
    Boy bows to the left hand girl; girl curtsies.
  3. "All join your paddies and circle the hall."
    All eight join hands and circle to the left.
  4. "Swing your honeys high and low, and the head lady get set to go."

1.   2.   3.   4.

  Boys swing their own partners at the home position.
  5. "The first lady swings the right hand gent with the right hand round, back to your honey with the left hand round, to the opposite gent with the right hand round, back to your partner with the left as you come down, and to the left hand gent with the right hand round, and back to your honey with the left, and the birdie in the center, and seven hands round."
    The first girl steps into the center of the set and turns to the second boy. He takes her by a right forearm grip, turns once

143

around, and leaves her facing her own partner. She swings her own partner with a left forearm grip, then swings the number three boy with the right. She swings with her own partner and then swings the number four boy with the right forearm grip, then back to swing with her own partner. After the last swing the first girl stands in the center of the set, and the other seven dancers join hands and circle to the left around her.

6. "Now the birdie hops out and the crow hops in; join your paddies and go it again."

The first girl steps back into the circle, her partner steps into the middle of the set, and the dancers circle to the left around him.

7. "The crow hops out with an allemande left."

As the circle moves around, the boy keeps his eye on his corner girl, steps out of the circle, joins left hands with her, walks all around her, and comes back to face his own partner.

8. "And a right to your partner, right and left grand."

The boys extend their right hands to their partners, pass them by, and give the coming girl their left hands. This continues until the boys reach their original partners across the square from their home spot.

9. "Promenade eight when you come straight."

Boys take their partners in a crossed hand skaters' position and walk in the line of direction to their home spot in the square.

10. "Now everyone swing your honeys high and low, and the second lady get set to go."

Variations:

The caller could call in Step 6. . . . . "The crow steps in and joins the wren; it's six hands up, and we'll go it again."

The caller might add a call after 6 and before 7: "Raise your hands way high in the air, and the crow (or bird) fly away to another square."

This call means that the seven in the circle raise their hands to form arches, while the center dancer goes under an arch and enters another circle to dance with another partner for the remainder of the dance.

Variations should not be used until dancers are familiar with the original form of the dance.

SCHOTTISCHE COUPLE DANCE—*Any good schottische may be used. Imperial 6035 (Balen I. Karlstad), 1046 (California Schottische); Linden 29 (Balen I. Karlstad)*

Formation:
Couples in double circle, facing counterclockwise, inside hands joined.

Directions:
Boy begins with the left foot, and the girl with the right foot. Directions are given for the boy; the girl does the counterpart.

1. Starting with the left foot, run 3 steps forward and hop on the left foot; extend the right foot slightly forward.

145

2. Repeat Step 1, starting with the right foot and hopping on it.
3. Join both hands with partner, turn to the left, and make one complete turn with 4 step-hops.

Variations:

Repeat Steps 1 and 2 of the Schottische Couple Dance step.

2.

1. On the turn the boy turns to his left, the girl to her right, and with 4 step-hops, each makes a small circle, returning to his partner.
2. On the turn, take partner in social dance position and make 2 complete turns with the 4 step-hops.
3. On the turn, the boy and girl face each other, join both hands, and do a dish-rag turn.
4. On the turn, the boy kneels; the girl joins right hands with her partner and does 4 step-hops around her partner.

3.

SCHOTTISCHE FOURSOME—*Imperial 1046; Linden 29*

Formation:

Couples in fours, facing counterclockwise, partners with inside hands joined, and front couple joined by outside hands with the couple directly behind.

1. a.

Directions:

1. Everyone begins with the left foot and does the Schottische Couple Dance step.
   a) Starting with the left foot, run 3 steps forward; hop on the left foot and extend the right foot slightly forward.
   b) Repeat a, starting with the right foot and hopping on it.

1. b.

146

2. The front couple release inside hands, and the boy turns to the left and goes around the rear couple. His partner turns to the right and goes around the rear couple, and they meet behind the back couple, join inside hands, and begin the steps again. The turn movement is done with 4 step-hops.

Variation:

Repeat step 1 of the Schottische Foursome. On the turn, the front couple moves backward with 4 step-hops under the arch formed by the joined hands of the back couple. The latter is then in the lead, but must do a dish-rag turn to be in the correct position.

SCHOTTISCHE STEP—*Imperial 6035, 1046; Linden 29*

Formation:

The Schottische may be taught in a line formation with the students facing the instructor, in a circle formation with hands joined, or, as some instructors have found it possible, in couples.

Directions:

Position: Social dance or open.

1. Run 3 steps forward, left, right, left, and hop on the fourth count. The hop is done on the left foot, while at the same time the right foot swings forward with the knee bent.

2. Repeat Step 1, beginning with the right foot and hopping on it.

3. Four step-hops: step on the left foot and hop on it while swinging the right foot forward with the knee bent. Repeat with the right, the left, and the right.

The 4 step-hops may be done in the line of direction in open position or with partners facing in the social dance position and making a turn to the boy's left.

147

Extremely vigorous, Seven Jumps is a Danish man's dance. One usually acts as a leader and dances in the center of the circle.

Formation:

Single circle facing center of floor.

Directions:

Much of the enjoyment of this dance comes during the time you wait for the music. There should be no movement, and the dancers should wait in suspense for the music to begin.

1. First Jump:
   a) Everyone joins hands and skips 8 steps to the left.
   b) Jump high, land on both feet, and skip 8 steps to the right.
   c) Place hands on hips, raise right foot, bend knee.

   d) On the first note, stamp right foot; on the next, stand motionless.

2. Second Jump:
   a) Everyone joins hands and skips 8 steps to the left.
   b) Jump high, land on both feet, and skip 8 steps to the right.

c) Place hands on hips, raise right foot, bend knee.

d) On the first note, stamp right foot; on the second, raise the left knee. Stamp the left foot on the next note, and remain motionless on the second.

3. Third Jump:

a) Everyone joins hands and skips 8 steps to the left.

b) Jump high, land on both feet, and skip 8 steps to the right.

c) Place hands on hips, raise right foot, bend knee.

d) Stamp right foot, then left foot. Kneel on the right knee and remain motionless.

4. Fourth Jump:

a) Everyone joins hands and skips 8 steps to the left.

b) Jump high, land on both feet, and skip 8 steps to the right.

c) Place hands on hips, raise right foot, bend knee.

d) Stamp right foot, then left foot.

e) Kneel on the right knee, then on both knees; remain motionless.

5. Fifth Jump:

a) Everyone joins hands and skips 8 steps to the left.

b) Jump high, land on both feet, and skip 8 steps to the right.

c) Place hands on hips, raise right foot, bend knee.

d) Stamp right foot, then left foot.

e) Kneel on the right knee, then on both knees.

f) Place right elbow on the floor and rest cheek on right palm; remain motionless.

6. Sixth Jump:
   a) Everyone joins hands and skips 8 steps to the left.
   b) Jump high, land on both feet, and skip 8 steps to the right.
   c) Place hands on hips, raise right foot, bend knee.
   d) Stamp right foot, then left foot.
   e) Kneel on the right knee, then on both knees.
   f) Place right elbow on the floor and rest cheek on right palm.
   g) Place left elbow on floor also; palms of both hands are at cheeks. Remain motionless.

7. Seventh Jump:
   a) Everyone joins hands and skips 8 steps to the left.
   b) Jump high, land on both feet, and skip 8 steps to the right.
   c) Place hands on hips, raise right foot, bend knee.
   d) Stamp right foot, then left foot.
   e) Kneel on the right knee, then on both knees.
   f) Place right elbow on the floor and rest cheek on right palm.
   g) Place left elbow on floor also; palms of both hands are at cheek.
   h) Bend down and touch forehead to floor.

THE THREAD FOLLOWS THE NEEDLE—*R.C.A. Victor 22760*

"The thread follows the needle,
  The thread follows the needle;
In and out the needle goes,
  As mother mends the children's clothes."

150

THREAD FOLLOWS
THE NEEDLE

Formation:

Single line formation; lines should be limited to 8 or 10 people, for longer lines take too long for enjoyment of the dance. Hands are joined.

Directions:

1. With a running step, the leader runs down the front of his line and passes under the raised arms of the last 2 people in the line.

2. Keeping their hands joined, the last 2 in the line face in the opposite direction after the leader has drawn the line under the arch. This crosses their arms on their chests and starts the "stitch."

3. The leader runs back to his original position, drawing the line after him, and then runs down the front of the line again, this time passing under under the arch of the next 2 at the foot of the line. They turn in place, and a "stitch" has been added. This continues and the song is repeated until all the children have turned to "stitches." The leader passes under his own arm at the last, and the chain is completed.

4. The children all drop hands quickly and face about, thus unraveling the stitches. The dance is repeated with a new leader.

1.

2.

3.

4.

1.

2.

3.

4.

Formation:

Groups of 3 in straight lines, one behind the other. Dancers have hands on each other's shoulders.

Directions:

The Troika is a Russian dance imitating prancing ponies and their coachman. The center dancer is the coachman. Prancing, light, spirited steps should be used throughout the dance.

1. Four light running steps diagonally to the right.
2. Four light running steps diagonally to the left.
3. Eight light running steps straight ahead.
4. Join hands in a straight line. Dancer on the right passes under the arms of the other 2 people and back to his own place; the person in the center turns under his own arm. The dancer on the left passes under the arms of the other dancers and around to place; the center person turns under his own arm.

Variations:

1. The sets of 3 may stand side by side and run 16 steps forward.
2. The dancer on the left may take 16 steps around the center dancer and the right hand dancer, rather than dancing under the arch formed by the 2 dancers.
3. After Step 4, the 2 outside dancers may join hands around the center dancer and circle with 16 running steps around him; they then raise their arms to form an arch and the center dancer runs under, and on to another group.

THE TWO-STEP—*2/4 or 4/4 Time—Any good two step record may be used. Folkraft 1035 (Oklahoma Mixer); Columbia 39386 (Syncopated Clock)*

Formation:

The two-step may be taught in a line formation with the students facing the instructor or in a circle formation with hands joined.

Directions:

Directions are given for the boys; the girls do the counterpart, beginning with the opposite foot. The step, when completed, is sometimes known as a "Two-step left." The two-step right is the same step beginning with the right foot.

1. Step forward with the left foot.
2. Bring the right foot forward to the left foot, and transfer the weight to the right foot.
3. Step the left foot forward.
4. Cue Calls:
   a) Left, together, left;
      Right, together, right,
   b) Two-step left and
      Two-step right.
5. Position: The two-step may be done in the social dance position or the open position.

THE WALTZ—*3/4 Time—Any good waltz record may be used. Windsor 7614 (Missouri); Decca 24535 (Missouri); Black Mountain 1001 (Medley Waltz); Victor 21-0489 (Whisper Waltz)*

The basic waltz steps are given here for the leader who desires to instruct elementary children in this dance. Several of the folk dances given in this section call for the waltz or two-step.

Formation:

Couples take social dancing position: all previously explained.

Directions for the Pursuit Waltz step:

Boys usually begin the dance step with the left foot. The description given is for the boy; the

153

girls do the counterpart. The fact that boys lead the dance should be emphasized by the instructor.

1. Slide the left foot forward.
2. Slide the right foot forward beyond the left foot.
3. Bring the feet together, and transfer the weight to the left foot.
4. Slide the right foot forward.
5. Slide the left foot forward beyond the right foot.
6. Bring the feet together and transfer the weight to the right foot.
7. Cue calls for the waltz step:
   a) *1, 2, 3*
       4, 5, 6
   b) Left, right, together;
       Right, left, together.

The backward movement is the same as the forward step. The dancers use a simple walking motion, starting back with the left foot.

For basic instruction purposes, two suggestions for teaching the formation are made. First, the dancers should stand in a line facing the instructor so that they may follow the footwork given. Secondly, the dancers join hands in a single circle, then turn and face in the line of direction. The entire circle will move smoothly if everyone is doing the step correctly.

SAFETY ON THE PLAYGROUND

A well-designed and well-supervised playground can be a safe place for children to play. Approximately one-third of all schoolyard accidents take place in unorganized activities; alert supervision can prevent many of these needless mishaps. Apparatus is involved in a large number of injuries below the fifth grade level, while athletic games take the largest toll in the upper grades. Apparatus which presents unusual hazards and is difficult to supervise should not be installed; safe equipment which meets the needs of the children should be used instead. The following is an outline of a practical safety program.

A. Teach safety practices to the children.
    1. Every individual is responsible for safety.
    2. All playground rules must be followed.
    3. General rules for the individual child:
        a) No child should attempt stunts beyond his ability.
        b) Point out the correct use of such apparatus as swings, teeters, giant strides, slides and Jungle Gyms.
        c) Only older children should use apparatus.
        d) Prohibit children from fighting for turns, jumping on moving equipment, and pushing and shoving around equipment.

4. The playground should be kept free of such hazards as broken glass, tin cans, and other rubbish.
   a) Prohibit the throwing of sand, rocks and sticks.
   b) Prohibit the use of slingshots, pea-shooters, etc.
   c) Keep rocks and sticks off the paved areas.
5. Teach children to know their limitations:
   a) Over-strenuous play is harmful to the child.
   b) A child should not participate in any game too hard for him.
   c) Playing for extended periods of time usually results in the player becoming less skillful and, subsequently, more prone to accident and injury.
6. Never use equipment in need of repair:
   a) Examine structures often: foundations and joinings.
   b) Grease and oil moving parts frequently.
7. Require that all accidents be reported immediately.
   a) Administer first aid when necessary.
   b) Report all accidents to the proper authorities.
B. Safety practices in the use of apparatus.
   1. Swings:
      a) Only one child to a swing.
      b) No swinging on the framework.
      c) Child should remain seated in the swing and should hold on to chains with both hands.
      d) No dismounting while swing is in motion.
      e) No running under moving swings.
      f) No high, dangerous swinging.
      g) Swingers should all face in the same direction.
      h) Non-swingers should remain at a safe distance from the swings.
      i) Strap or bucket type seats are preferable.

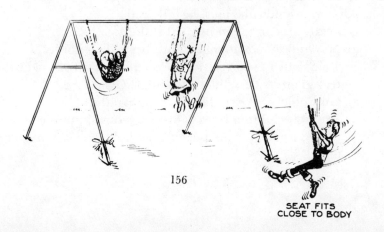

156

SEAT FITS
CLOSE TO BODY

PULLING PERSON
FROM SWING

RUNNING UNDER
MOVING SWING

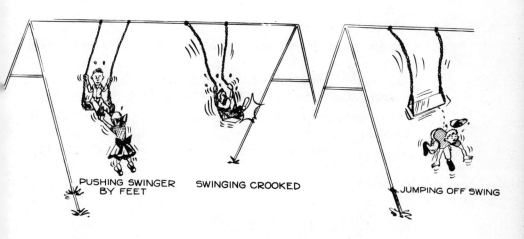

PUSHING SWINGER
BY FEET

SWINGING CROOKED

JUMPING OFF SWING

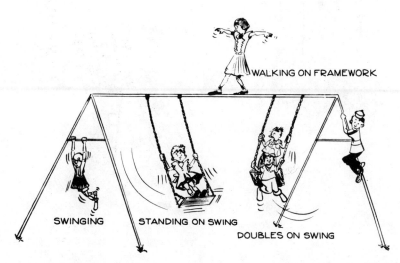

WALKING ON FRAMEWORK

SWINGING

STANDING ON SWING

DOUBLES ON SWING

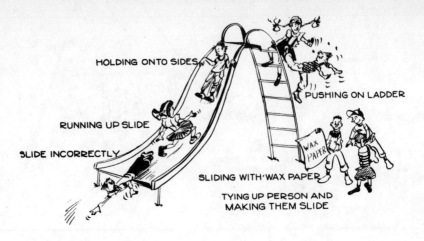

HOLDING ON TO SIDES
PUSHING ON LADDER
RUNNING UP SLIDE
SLIDE INCORRECTLY
WAX PAPER
SLIDING WITH WAX PAPER
TYING UP PERSON AND
MAKING THEM SLIDE

2. Slides:
   a) Sliding position: feet first, legs together, in a sitting position.
   b) Foot of the slide should always be kept clear.
   c) No small children on a slide unless an adult is present.
   d) Guard against the use of wax bread wrappers to make the slide slick.
   e) Sliders should ascend the slide only by means of the ladder.

INSPECT ALL EQUIPMENT

158

3. Teeters:
   a) Children should face each other while teetering.
   b) No standing on the board.
   c) Dismounting: the first child should leave the board slowly and carefully, thus permitting his partner to dismount safely.
   d) Players should keep feet from under board.

HOLD TEETER CAREFULLY

DO NOT BUMP

4. Giant strides:
   a) No small children.
   b) Child should hold on to ladder rung and not place feet through the rungs.
   c) Child should work toward center pole and wait for the stride to stop.

5. Rings:
   a) Travel should be in one direction.
   b) Have players grip rings tightly.
   c) No feet through rings.
   d) Do not use rings when they are wet.
   e) No small children.

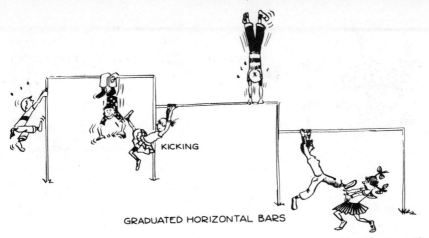

KICKING

GRADUATED HORIZONTAL BARS

6. Horizontal bars, horizontal ladder, catwalk climbers, and climbing apparatus:
   a) No jumping off from high positions.
   b) Teach children proper grips and leverage.
C. Safety practices on the ball field.
   1. Be sure the children know and follow the rules of the game.
   2. Teach the use of such safety equipment as catchers' masks, body protectors, and glasses shields.
   3. Warn players against chasing balls into the street without proper caution.
   4. Require players to stand behind the backstop while waiting for turn at bat; also, keep spectators at a safe distance.
   5. Teach correct usage of the bat:
      a) It should be held with the mark facing up.
      b) Player should not throw the bat after hitting the ball.
      c) The bat handle should be taped to provide better gripping surface.
   6. Emphasize control when throwing the ball.
   7. Have players in the field call for the ball, in order to avoid collisions.

J'T THROW BAT   AVOID THROWING BALL TOO HARD

CALL FOR BALL

WATCH WHERE YOU ARE THROWING

DO NOT CHASE BALL INTO STREET

D. Safety practices in tag games.
  1. Limit the area of play, and make sure that it is far enough from such hazards as traffic, water, etc.
  2. Prohibit rough play.
E. Safety practices in the gym.
  1. Players should have gym shoes, and should tie shoes securely.
  2. Avoid the use of pins in gym clothing.
  3. Use mats for protection when necessary.
  4. Do not use wax on gym floor.
F. Safety practices in the locker room.
  1. Keep locked when not in use.
  2. Have children keep it neat.

162

JUNGLE GYM, CLIMBING TOWER, CASTLE TOWER, AND CLIMBING MAZE GAMES

Climbing apparatus appeals to the children. It gives them the opportunity to develop their shoulder and arm muscles and body control. As the children learn the use of the apparatus, they should be encouraged to play games and perform stunts.

1. Tag: players climb over climbing apparatus to avoid being tagged.
    a) Elimination tag: as each player is tagged, he leaves the game; the last player tagged is "it" for the next game.
    b) Safety tag: played as ordinary tag with certain zones on the apparatus set aside as "safe." Players in these zones cannot be tagged.
2. Relays: players climb to the top and back to their lines. The first team to finish wins the relay.
3. Stunts:
    a) Chinning: player grasps the bar with his hands and pulls himself up until his chin touches the bar.
    b) Lay out: player locks his feet around the inner cross bars and holds on to the upright bars; he then goes back in a lay out position. This stunt should be done on the lower level so the performer can untangle his feet. If he is not able to come to a sitting position, he places his hands on the ground and unhooks his feet.

HORIZONTAL LADDER

JUMPING

PIKES PEAK

LIGHTHOUSE TOWER

164

TEAM GAMES

Team games are concerned primarily with specific, complex skills which help to develop strength, agility, endurance, and dexterity. Team activities are an integral part of the physical education program, and most children desire to take an active part in the traditionally established games. Through team games and good leadership, there will be many opportunities for teaching and encouraging desirable social, mental, and emotional qualities in the individual child, as well as in guiding the child in developing such wholesome attitudes of behavior as good sportsmanship, loyalty, cooperation with fellow teammates, self-control, and the desire to play according to the rules.

The objectives of team games are:

1. To provide games suited to the age group and its physical development.
2. To allow the individual child to participate in activities with other children of the same ability and experience.
3. To provide, through varied game situations, the opportunity to live and learn by doing, and to develop such social qualities as fair play, loyalty, self-control, courage, friendliness, courtesy, obedience, sportsmanship, and the desire to play according to the rules.
4. To develop in the child a responsive attitude toward the performing of skills and techniques.
5. To provide games which vary in degree of difficulty and thus meet the capacities of all children.
6. To develop enthusiasm and interest in group activities.
7. To provide opportunities for neuro-muscular development.
8. To develop safe habits with regard to equipment, playing area, personal limitations, and fellow players.
9. To provide instructional periods in a variety of sports, which are to be used in the inter-school and intramural program.
10. To provide opportunities for officiating team games, thus developing a good attitude toward game officials.

TEACHING OF SKILLS

It is a recognized principle of teaching that interest is an important factor in the learning process; it is the driving force behind learning and is increased if that experience is satisfying. Therefore, it is important that the teacher be able to capture the child's interest and expound the fundamentals of the game through it. The child's concern with any sport will be greatest during that particular sport's season, when he sees many pictures and write-ups in daily newspapers and magazines of the sport stars, team schedules, and individual standings and averages.

The beginner in a team sport should progress first through a series of lead up games, which, when placed together, actually make up the game in question. The drill period grows out of the demand of the player, and is the most effective learning period because the individual is ready to correct his errors. The effective use of relays, contests and lead-up games has meaning to the player, and he enters into them with enthusiasm and active interest.

In teaching a drill, give the beginner a chance to get the feel of the skill being taught by going through it slowly, then stepping up the speed as the group becomes familiar with the pattern. When definite progress is being made by the group, satisfaction develops, learning becomes easier, and drills are accepted as necessary. It is very important that suitable drills be used to meet the needs and the abilities of the children being taught, for if a child sees he is not making progress, he loses interest or becomes a disciplinary problem. Therefore, the instruction should be so organized that it meets the needs of the individual child.

The range of abilities in a class may be wide, for there are children who lack physical coordination in doing things with their hands and feet. Special effort and attention should be given to these children; they must not feel that they are being left out of the group or that they are holding up its progress. The teacher should build up the child's confidence through sympathetic understanding of his handicap. Patience, encouragement, and praise go a long way toward helping the slow player gain self-confidence. Demonstrations by skillful players or the teacher give the children a much better mental picture of the drill pattern than a verbal explanation or description.

When working with small children, it is best to select equipment that they can handle efficiently without being awkward in its use. Balls should fit their hands and be light in weight, so that they can imitate

166

the movements of the demonstration without going through unnecessary motion.

When skills are woven into drills, relays, and lead-up games, the activity is interesting and the experience of improving playing ability increases the child's desire to become more efficient through practice.

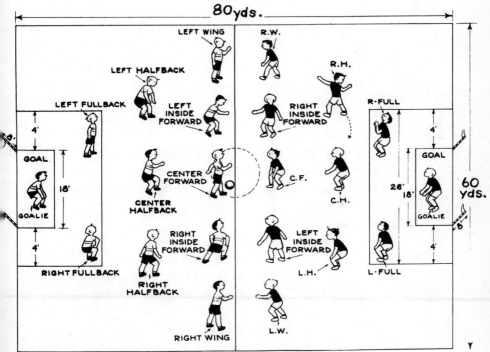

MODIFIED SOCCER

PLAYING FIELD: Playfield 60 yds. x 80 yds.

EQUIPMENT: Soccer ball, colored jerseys, tennis shoes, and goal posts.

NUMBER OF PLAYERS: 22.

FORMATION: See diagram.

RULES OF THE GAME:*

I. Positions.
  A. Goalkeeper (Goalie).
    1. Defends goal; remains in goal area as a defense player.
    2. Should have skill in handling the ball with his hands, as he is the only player who may use his hands to defend the goal.
    3. Goalkeeper may, while within the goal area, do the following:
      a) Catch the ball.
      b) Bounce the ball.
      c) Combine a bounce or a juggle with a punt or a throw.
      d) Juggle the ball once by throwing or tapping it into the air before throwing the ball.
      e) Fist the ball with one or both fists.
      f) Pick up the ball.
      g) Punt the ball.
      h) Take not more than 4 steps while holding the ball.
      i) Tap or throw the ball above and over the crossbar.
      j) Throw the ball.
    4. May be charged when in possession of the ball.
  B. Fullbacks.
    1. There are 2 fullbacks on each team.
    2. Fullbacks play in front and on each side of the goal.
    3. Fullbacks are defensive players and should not go past the center line.
  C. Halfbacks.
    1. There are 3 halfbacks on each team.
    2. Halfbacks play offensively and defensively.
      a) Retreat and help defend when opponents have ball.
      b) Advance with ball when in own possession.
  D. Forwards.
    1. There are 5 forwards on each team.
      a) Center and 2 inside forwards are mainly offensive players and seldom retreat into deep defensive territory.
      b) Two outside forwards, "wings": play the sides of the field, are foot passers, advance the ball, score or pass to other forwards and to halfbacks, and seldom retreat far into defensive half of field.

* Official rules, National Collegiate Athletic Bureau, Soccer Guide, N.Y.

II. The game.
   A. The object of the game is to kick the ball through the opponents' goal.
   B. The ball may be advanced by kicking, dribbling, heading and chesting, or players may use shoulders, hips, or legs.
   C. The ball must be advanced by kicking and cannot be touched by the hands or arms except when throwing it in from out of bounds.

III. Playing time.
   A. Four 6 minute quarters.
   B. Two-minute rest periods between quarters.
   C. Ten-minute rest period between halves.
   D. Teams change goals at the end of first, second, and third quarters.

IV. Start of the game.
   A. Official flips a coin to determine which team has the choice of the kickoff or the end of the field.
   B. The game is started with a place kick from the center of the field.
      1. Receiving team must be at least 10' from the ball.
      2. No player on the kicking team may pass the middle line before the kick.
      3. After the kick off, players may be either ahead of or behind the ball.
      4. The ball must travel not less than its circumference to be a legal kick.
      5. The player taking the kick may not touch the ball again until another player plays it.
   C. After a goal is made, the team scored against kicks off.

V. Dead ball or ball out of play.
   A. A ball that has left the playing field by rolling or traveling through the air.
   B. After a temporary suspension of the game, in which no goal, foul, or touch was involved, the game is started when the official drops the ball to the ground at the spot where play was suspended.

VI. Fouls.
   A. Touching the ball intentionally or accidentally, with any part of the hands or arms by any player other than the goalkeeper.

STRIKING   PUSHING   HOLDING

B. Pushing, holding, blocking, tripping, striking, shouldering, charging from behind.

TRIPPING   SHOULDERING   CHARGING FROM BEHIND

C. Technical evasion.
   1. Being off side.
   2. Playing ball the second time before it has been touched or played by another player following a throw-in, penalty kick, or free kick.
   3. Not facing field of play and keeping both feet on the ground when taking throw-in.
   4. Touching ball before it touches ground after it has been dropped by the official.
   5. Goalkeeper carrying the ball, or taking more than 4 steps while holding the ball.
   6. Improperly charging a goalkeeper.
      a) Goalkeeper may be charged when he holds the ball, when he is obstructing an opponent, and when he is not within the goal area.
      b) Play must not be intentionally rough or over-aggressive.

VII. Out of bounds.
   A. When a ball touches or crosses the side lines.
      1. It is thrown in at that spot by a player of the team opposite the one who touched it last.
      2. The ball must be thrown in over the head with both hands, and the feet must not leave the ground on the throw.
      3. The ball must touch another player before the thrower can again touch it.

VIII. Goal kick.
   A. Is awarded to a member of the defending team when a member of the attacking team kicks the ball over a goal line, but not between the goal posts.
   B. The defending team places the ball on the goal line at the point where it passed over the goal line.
      1. No opponent may be within 10 yards of the ball until it has been kicked.
      2. The kicker may not touch the ball until a second player has touched it.
      3. The goalie or fullback usually place-kicks the ball.

IX. Free kick.
   A. Is a penalty kick for touching the ball with the hands or arms, for tripping, blocking, shoving, or charging an opponent from behind.
   B. The ball is placed on the field at the spot of the foul, and the team fouled is allowed to place-kick the ball.
   C. Opponents must remain at least 10 yards away.

X. Corner kick.
   A. Is awarded to an attacking team if a member of the defending team intentionally or accidentally kicks the ball over the goal line, but not between the goal posts.
   B. The ball is placed on the ground at one corner of the field and is kicked across in front of the goal, where the forwards attempt to score.

XI. Time out.
   A. Is taken when ball is out of play.
   B. Two time outs will be allowed each team during a game.

XII. Scoring.
   A. Each goal made counts 1 point.
   B. A goal does not count when:
      1. Ball is carried through by members of the attacking team.
      2. Ball is thrown across goal area.
      3. Ball is knocked through by the action of the arms or hands.

XIII. Terminology.
   A. Attacking team: the team in possession of the ball and attempting to put it over the opponents' goal line.

B. Blocking: intercepting the progress of the ball by the use of any part of the body other than arms and hands.

C. Defending: not in possession of the ball, attempting to keep the ball from crossing own goal line.

D. Dribbling: kicks which propel the ball forward and at the same time keep it near the feet so that the player does not lose control of it.

E. Goal line: end line of the playing area.

F. Heading: meeting the ball with the front or the side of the head.

G. Juggling: throwing the ball or tapping it into the air and then catching it before it can touch the ground; only the goalkeeper may juggle the ball.

H. Punt: a kick made by dropping the ball and kicking it before it strikes the ground; only the goalkeeper, within his own penalty zone, may punt the ball.

I. Shouldering: using the shoulder to propel or direct the ball; no part of the arms may contact the ball.

J. Touch line: side lines of the playing area.

K. Trapping: stopping the ball's progress by use of the foot on top of the ball, or by using front of the legs, knees bent, and the ground.

MODIFIED SOCCER FOR GIRLS

PLAYING FIELD: Playfield 60 yds. x 80 yds.

EQUIPMENT: Same as for boys.

NUMBER OF PLAYERS: 22.

FORMATION: See diagram.

RULES OF THE GAME:* Soccer rules for girls are similar to the boys' rules in general play and in manner of scoring. In the girls' rules, no body contact is allowed. The 5 players in the foward line are: half backs, right and left centers, center; behind them are the full backs, and goalkeeper. When a team takes a kickoff, the 5 players in the forward line must stand back of the restraining line. The defending team is in a similar position in their half of the field, but all players are behind the half-way line.

* National Section for Girls and Women's Sports by American Association for Health and Physical Education and Recreation; 1201 Sixteenth St. N.W., Washington 6, D.C.

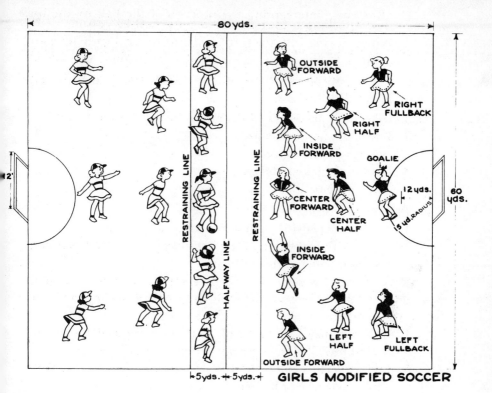

GIRLS MODIFIED SOCCER

I. Start game:

    A. The referee tosses a coin to decide the choice of goal and kick-off; the captain that wins the toss may have the option of kick-off or choice of goals.

        1. At the beginning of each quarter thereafter, the kickoff is made by the team which did not kickoff at the beginning of the previous quarter.

        2. Teams shall exchange goals at halftime.

    B. The ball is placed into play by a kickoff from the center of the field in the direction of the opponents' goal.

        1. The ball must travel into the opponents' territory at least the distance of its own circumference.

        2. The player who kicked the ball may not touch the ball again until it has first been touched by another player.

        3. No opponent may cross the restraining line and no team-mate of the kicking team may cross the halfway line until the ball has been kicked.

173

4. The attacking team may advance the ball by passing, dribbling, kicking with the feet, or hitting the ball with any part of their bodies except their hand or arms (may use folded arms across the chest when blocking or trapping with that part of the body).

C. Goalkeeper's privileges while within her own penalty area.
1. Use her hands on the ball.
2. Bounce the ball once.
3. Punt or drop kick the ball.
4. Throw the ball.

D. Players' privileges.
1. A player may dribble, shoulder, or head the ball.
2. A player in possession of the ball may place herself between her opponent and the ball.
3. A player may stop the ball by trapping it under her foot, between her feet, or between the front of her legs and the ground.
4. A player may kick the ball while it is trapped by an opponent provided she does not commit a foul.
5. Any player may stop the ball by blocking it with any part of her body except her hands and arms.

E. Fouls.
1. A foul is an infringement of the rules of the game for which a free kick or penalty kick is awarded the opponents.
   a) A player may not push, trip, kick, hold, strike, or charge her opponent.
   b) Carrying is a foul committed by the goalkeeper by taking more than 2 steps while holding the ball.
   c) Handling is a foul committed by a player striking, or propelling the ball with the hand or any part of the arm between the wrist and the shoulder.
2. A player is off-side if she is nearer her opponents' goal line than the ball at the moment it is played by one of her own team unless she is in her own half of the field, or unless there are 3 of her opponents nearer their own goal line than she is.
   a) A player shall not be penalized for being off-side unless she is playing the ball, interfering with another player, or gaining some advantage from standing in an off-side position.

    b) Once off-side, a player can be put inside only if she is behind the ball when it is played by one of her own team, or if there are 3 opponents between her and their goal line when the ball is played by one of her own team farther from her opponents' goal than she is.

    c) A free kick is awarded as a penalty for off-side, but a goal cannot be scored directly in the kick.

F. Penalties.
1. Free kicks are awarded as penalties for any foul committed outside a team's own penalty area.
2. When a free kick is awarded, a place kick is taken from the spot where the foul occurred.

    a) All opponents must be 6 yards away.

    b) The kick must travel the circumference of the ball.

    c) The kicker may not play the ball until it has been touched by another player.

3. Penalty kicks are awarded for the following fouls committed by the defending team in its own penalty area:

    a) Trapping, holding, pushing, striking, charging an opponent.

    b) Handling the ball.

    c) Goalkeeper carrying the ball.

4. When a penalty kick is awarded in the goal area, a place kick shall be taken from the penalty kick mark, 12 yards from the goal; the ball must be kicked by an attacking player.

    a) The player taking the penalty kick must kick it forward and attempt to send it between the goal posts.

    b) All players, with the exception of the player taking the penalty kick and the opposing goalkeeper, must be outside the penalty area and in the field of play.

    c) The opponent goalkeeper may stand on the goal line but must not advance beyond it until the ball has been kicked.

G. Scoring.
1. Field goal, 2 points.

    a) A field goal is scored when the ball has been kicked or legally given impetus with the body so that it passes over the goal line between the posts and under the cross bar.

b) A field goal may be scored from any spot on the playing field by a player who is inside.

2. Penalty kick, 1 point.
    a) A penalty kick is scored when the ball passes over the goal line between the goal posts and under the cross bar.
    b) The ball must be kicked at the penalty kick mark by a player taking the penalty kick.

H. Out-of-bounds.
    1. When a ball goes over the side lines, a player of the opposite team to that which caused the ball to go out-of-bounds shall use a place kick to send it into the field in any direction from the point on the side line where it left the field of play.
        a) The player kicking the ball must stand outside the field of play.
        b) The ball shall be considered in play as soon as it has been kicked.
        c) All opponents must be 5 yards away until the ball has been kicked.
        d) The ball must be touched by another player before the kicker can play the ball.
        e) A goal may not be scored from a kickin.

I. Playing time.
    1. Four quarters, 6 to 8 minutes in each quarter.
    2. Two minutes between the first and second quarter and the third and fourth quarters.
    3. Ten minutes between halves.
    4. Time out can be taken only when the ball is out of play or in the case of injury.
    5. Two time-outs will be allowed each team during the game.

J. Terminology (refer to the terminology used in Boys' Soccer Rules).
    1. Attackers: the team in possession of the ball, attempting to make a goal.
    2. Dribbling: carrying the ball with slight successive kicks so that the dribbler keeps control of the ball.
    3. Defenders: the team which does not have possession of the ball and which attempts to stop a goal from being made across their goal line or attempts to gain possession of the ball.

4. Own goal: members of a team stand at the kick-off with their backs toward their own goal. Each goalkeeper protects his own goal.
5. Own half of field: that half of the field between the half-way line and the goal line on which the team's goal is located.

SOCCER TECHNIQUE AND FUNDAMENTALS

I. Inside foot dribble.
  A. Position of foot.
    1. The leg and foot are rotated outward, and the inside of foot meets the ball.
    2. Arms are free for balance.
    3. Dribbler should use split vision (peripheral): he must watch the ball and see the field in front, so that opponents or teammates may be spotted and play can be planned ahead.

  B. Action.
    1. The ball should be tapped or pushed along the ground with the inside of either foot.
    2. The weight of the body should be forward, head toward the ball.
    3. Feet should alternate in playing the ball.
    4. The ball should travel in a straight line.
    5. The ball should not get too far ahead; keep it near feet for control (12"–15").
    6. Push, do not kick ball.

C. Follow-through: the body weight follows-through with the playing foot.
  1. Playing foot steps forward in a normal step (toe straight ahead).
  2. Push right foot, step right-left-right, tap left, step left-right-left.
D. Uses of inside foot dribble.
  1. Advancing the ball while running.
  2. Defending the goal when opponents are pressing.
  3. Moving the ball when control is worth more than speed.

II. Outside foot dribble: the ball is pushed with the outside of the foot at the area of the small toe.
  A. Position.
    1. The foot is rotated inward so that the outside of the foot is in a position to meet the ball.
    2. The arms are free for balance.

  B. Action.
    1. The ball is played with the same foot with every second step; push ball with right and step right-left; push ball with right, follow through with right, etc.
    2. Keep ball close to feet for ball control (12″–15″).
    3. Keep eye on ball while playing the ball.

C. Follow-through: the body weight follows through on the kicking foot, which rotates to normal position before follow-through step is completed.

D. Uses of outside foot dribble.
  1. Keeps the body between an opponent and the ball.
  2. Facilitates faking and dodging.
  3. Makes a fast dribble possible.

III. Heading (straight ahead).
  A. Position.
    1. A standing, feet slightly apart, jump stance.
    2. Play in motion: player takes off on one foot like a broad-jumper, driving from the hip, knee, ankle, and foot.
    3. Arms should swing free at the sides.

  B. Action.
    1. Jumping into the air and meeting the ball gives added impetus to the ball.
    2. The head should be brought back and then forward quickly, hitting the ball with the forehead at the hair line: the chin should be tucked in as the head is brought forward.
  C. Follow-through.
    1. Trunk should be inclined forward.
    2. The head follows through as much as possible by stretching forward away from the shoulders in the direction of the headed ball.

179

D. Coaching suggestions.
   1. Keep eyes on the ball as long as possible.
   2. Time the jump with the flight of the ball and meet it as high as possible in the air.
   3. Do not duck the head or wait for the ball to fall on the head.
   4. Do not try to head a ball below the chest height; another player may attempt to kick at the ball at the same time.
E. Uses of heading.
   1. Places the ball away from an opponent.
   2. Gains better control of the ball.
   3. Gets the ball to teammates.
   4. Scoring and defense.

IV. Instep kick.
   A. Position.
      1. The kicking leg should swing back from the hip, the knee bent with the heel well back, and the toes pointing toward the ground.
      2. Arms should be free at the sides for balance.
      3. The weight should be on the non-kicking foot.
      4. The ball should be slightly forward of the kicking foot.

B. Action.
    1. The kicking leg should be swung forward to meet the ball as the leg straightens, meeting the ball with the top of the instep, the toe of the kicking foot pointing downward.
    2. The body should be over the ball.
    3. The force of the kick comes with the knee action.
    4. The kicking leg and ankle should be relaxed until just before the impact with the ball.
C. Follow-through.
    1. The leg should follow-through in the direction of the kick with the toe pointing upward.
    2. The trunk should be bent forward slightly.
    3. Arms should be out at sides to maintain balance.
D. Uses of the instep kick.
    1. Long passes.
    2. Long goal kicks: free kicks and place kicks.
    3. Keeping the ball moving in the same direction the player is traveling.
    4. Returning a ball traveling toward you to the opposite direction.
E. Coaching suggestions.
    1. Keep eye on the ball.
    2. Keep kicking leg and ankle relaxed.
    3. Keep toe pointed toward ground so that the instep comes in contact with the ball; ball should remain low in flight.

V. Punching or striking by the goalkeeper.
A. Position.
    1. Feet spread slightly.
    2. Arm up, elbow flexed, hand clenched.
    3. Trunk should be inclined slightly forward.

B. Action.
  1. Ball is hit with the clenched fist.
  2. The impetus comes from the forward swing of the arms and the snap of the wrist.
  3. Jump to meet the ball.
C. Follow-through.
  1. Arms follow-through with the strike.
  2. Trunk comes forward with the striking motion.
  3. Both feet come to the ground together.
D. Coaching suggestions.
  1. Two fists are better than one.
  2. Eyes must follow the ball.
E. Uses of punching and striking.
  1. When surrounded by offensive players.
  2. When there is not enough time to catch the ball.
  3. To deflect the ball coming from a sharp angle.

VI. Inside kick.
  A. Position.
    1. The ball is kicked with the inside of the instep of the kicking foot.
    2. Weight should be on the non-kicking foot.
    3. The kicking leg should swing from the hip, knee slightly bent and ankle relaxed.

  B. Action.
    1. Keep eye on the ball at all times.
    2. Arms should be relaxed.
    3. The leg swings forward toward the direction of the kick.

C. Follow-through.
  1. After the kick, the leg follows-through.
  2. Hip rotates slightly in the direction of the kick.
  3. End the kick with a step in the direction of the kick.
D. Uses for inside kick.
  1. Most accurate short kick.
  2. Passing at any angle.
  3. Shooting a goal shot where accuracy is needed.

VII. Outside kick.
  A. Position.
    1. The kicker's weight should be on the non-kicking foot.

  B. Action.
    1. The kicking leg should swing across in front of the non-kicking leg in a pendulum motion.
    2. With a quick motion, the kicking foot moves away from the supporting foot causing the ball to be pushed rather than kicked.
  C. Follow-through: after the kick, the leg should follow through, ending with a side step in the direction of the kick.
  D. Uses for the outside kick.
    1. For short quick passes.
    2. Used for deception in dribbling and passing.

VIII. Chest trapping.
    A. Position: Relaxed and bent slightly forward at the waist
       as the ball hits the chest.

    B. Action.
       1. The player moves forward as the ball hits the chest,
          ready to play the ball in any direction he wishes.
       2. After hitting the chest, the ball should drop at the feet
          or within one step.
    C. Coaching suggestions.
       1. Keep arms away from body and keep hands from touch-
          ing the ball.
       2. Relax when ball hits.
       3. Keep eyes on the ball.
    D. Uses of chest trapping.
       1. Stopping a bounding, kicked, or passed ball.
       2. Gaining control of the ball.

IX. Throw in.
  A. Position.
    1. The ball is held with the palms of the hands on opposite sides of the ball, fingers slightly spread, gripping the ball toward the back; thumbs are behind the ball.
    2. The arms are raised over the head, elbows bent with the wrists bent slightly downward so that the ball is held behind the head.

       The wrists, elbows, shoulders, and trunk all enter into the throw.
    3. Trunk should be inclined slightly backward with a slight arch in back.
    4. One foot should be ahead of the other (stride position) to maintain balance.
    5. The knees should be relaxed.

  B. Action.
    1. The distance of the throw depends upon the snap of muscles used in the throw.
    2. Arms are swung forward and downward with the elbows and wrists straightening during the throw.
    3. The trunk and knees straighten, and the weight is transferred to the ball of the forward foot.

C. Follow-through.
   1. The arms follow-through with the throw.
   2. Trunk should extend well forward.
   3. Back toe should remain on ground with weight on ball of front foot.
D. Coaching suggestions.
   1. Thrower should conceal the direction of throw.
   2. Thrower should turn waist as throw starts and pivot on toes.
   3. Lead the receiver if he is moving.
   4. Wing forwards and wing halfbacks should practice throw in.
   5. Avoid lob passes for short throw in.
   6. Make up your mind whether you are going to throw the ball at the receiver's feet, or body.
   7. Stress keeping feet on the ground.

DRILLS

CIRCLE DRIBBLE DRILL

FORMATION:　　　　　　See diagram.

RULES OF THE DRILL: At a given signal, number one player dribbles around the circle, back to his original position, and passes the ball to the player on his right. The drill is continued until all players have dribbled around the circle.

Team competition: Form 2 or more circles, each representing a team. At a given signal, the first player on each team starts the dribble around the circle, back to his original position, and gives the ball to the man to his right. The first team to complete its dribble wins.

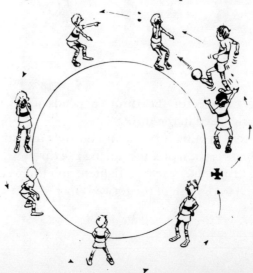

PASS AND TRAP DRILL.

FORMATION: See diagram.

RULES OF THE DRILL: Divide players into groups of 4 and 8. Number one player passes to number two player, who traps the ball and passes back to number one. Number one then passes to number three, etc. down the line to the last player.

Rotation: 1 to 2, 2 to 3, etc. Number six takes one's place. Each player takes the place as the lead man.

SOCCER DRILLS

FORMATION: See diagram.

RULES OF THE DRILL: Players form 2 lines, 20 to 30 feet apart, depending upon their skill. Use the following drills and combinations.

Types of Drills

Overhead pass	Stomach trap
Chest trap	Inside foot pass
Outside foot pass	Heading
Foot trap	

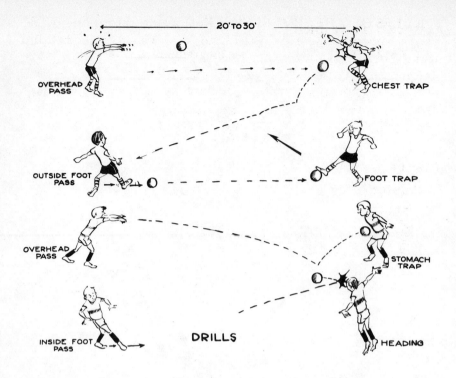

DRILLS

Combinations: Chest trap, instep kick or head; inside foot pass, trap, lob pass; instep kick, outside foot pass.

THROW-IN, HEAD, PASS, AND TRAP DRILL

FORMATION: See diagram.

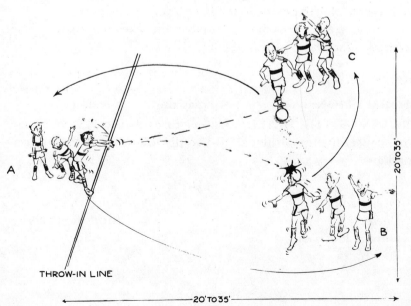

RULES OF THE DRILL: "A" line player throws in to "B" player, who heads the ball to "C." Line "C" player traps the ball and uses the outside foot pass to "A" line.

Rotation: "A" to "B," "B" to "C," "C" to "A." Reverse direction of throw-in, "A" to "C," "C" to "B," "B" to "A." "C" heads to "B," "B" traps and uses the inside foot pass to A line.

LEAD-UP GAMES

CIRCLE KICK

FORMATION: See diagram.

RULES OF THE GAME: Two to four players are designated as retrievers. At a given signal, the soccer ball is kicked around the circle. To keep the ball from leaving the circle, the players may use any part of the body to block it. If the ball leaves the circle between 2 players, these players exchange places with the 2 retrievers, and must await their turn to come back into the circle. If the ball goes between the legs of one player, he exchanges places with the retriever next in line.

If a kicker kicks a ball out over the shoulders of the players in the circle, the kicker must leave the circle and become a retriever. He stays a retriever until another player receives the same penalty, and they exchange places. If the same person makes more than 3 kicks over the shoulders of the players in the circle, he must leave the game.

KICK BALL

FORMATION: See diagram.

KICK BALL

RULES OF THE GAME: Divide · the players into 2 equal teams. Number each player and place the players on a softball field as the diagram indicates. The team kicking first is determined by the toss of a coin.

Kicker: player stands within the 6' circle. The kicker must kick any ball that rolls within the circle. If he fails to kick a ball that has been rolled inside the circle, a strike will be called. If 4 balls are called (ball rolled outside 6' circle), the kicker receives a free kick from the kick circle. The kicker goes to first base when the ball has been kicked fair. The kicker is out when:

1. He has 3 strikes,
2. He is thrown out at first,
3. He is tagged by a fielder before he reaches first base,
4. A fly ball is caught, fair or foul,

190

5. A supporting foot is not within the circle when the ball is kicked.
6. A foul ball is kicked on a free kick.

Base runner: player goes to first on the kicked fair ball (fair ball is any ball kicked within the first base line and third base line). The runner may advance to another base when:

1. A fielder overthrows a base.
2. There is a pass ball.
3. He is able to steal the next base or bases after a pitched ball has entered the kicking circle.
4. A fly ball has been caught; he may advance after the catch.
5. Forced by another base runner.

Runner is out when:
1. He leaves base before kicked ball has passed through the circle.
2. He is forced out by another runner taking his base.
3. He fails to reach the base before a player with the ball touches the base.
4. He leaves the base on a fly ball and base is touched by a player with the ball before he can return, or is tagged by a fielder with the ball while off base.
5. He passes another base runner or touches a base which is occupied by another player.
6. Interfering with a fielder attempting to field a ball.
7. He fails to touch a base while running the bases; the fielder may tag him with the ball, or tag the missed base before player returns.

Length of Game: 5 or 7 innings, or the class period. If there is not sufficient time to complete the full inning, the score shall revert to the last full inning unless the team at bat in the last half of the inning is ahead.

Scoring: a run scores when a player of the batting team circles the bases and returns home safely.

The game may be played with more than 9 players.

1. With 10, place at short stop between 1st and 2nd.
2. With 11, place in short center field.
3. With 12, place in field.
4. Over 24, players divide into 4 teams.

LINE SOCCER

PLAYING FIELD: Gymnasium, playfield; adjust the field to the group.

EQUIPMENT: Soccer ball.

NUMBER OF PLAYERS: 10–30.

FORMATION: See diagram.

RULES OF THE GAME: Divide into 2 equal teams, 2 players from each team acting as forwards. All other players act as goal keepers, and stand on their goal line to prevent the ball from crossing their goal line. The ball is placed in the middle of the field. The 4 forwards stand 5'–10' from the center; at a signal from the referee, they rush the ball and play as in soccer, each trying to kick the ball through the opponents' line. The ball must go through the line below the shoulders of the opponents.

The players on the goal line may stop the ball with any part of the body including the hands, or may bat or kick the ball back into the field. They can not catch or throw the ball.

After a score had been made by either team, the forwards rotate with the goalkeepers. If a score has not been made within 2 minutes, the referee calls time and the forwards rotate.

Fouls:

1. Forward touching the ball with the hands.
2. Guard advancing beyond the goal restraining line.
3. Ball going over the goalkeepers' heads.

Penalty:

Free kick from the spot of the foul by the offended team.

Out of bounds:

When the ball is kicked out of bounds by one team, the other team shall kick in bounds with a free kick. In case of a doubt as to who caused the ball to go out of bounds, the referee puts the ball on the center line for a center kick as in the illustration.

Score:

1 point for each time the ball passes the goalkeepers below the shoulders.

LONG BASE SOCCER

PLAYING FIELD:	Baseball field; may be smaller for lower grades.
EQUIPMENT:	Soccer ball and 2 bases.
NUMBER OF PLAYERS:	6 to 12 players per team.
FORMATION:	See diagram.

30' TO 40'

RULES OF THE GAME: The team in the field arranges itself as illustrated. The members of the batting team take turns kicking the soccer ball from home base into the field. They either may place the ball on home plate and kick, or have the ball rolled to them by a pitcher. There is no limit to the number of "strikes," but every "hit" is fair even though it may be only a foul tip. The batter stays up until he gets a hit.

After a hit, the batter must get to long base before the ball or before he is tagged. He may stay there or try to return to home base. Several persons may stay on long base at once as long as a batter is left. When more than one are on long base, they may not return home until a hit is made. Each player who gets home scores 1 point. The team at bat continues until 3 outs are made. A runner is out when:

1. A fielder catches a fly hit by him.
2. A fielder gets a ball and tags either long base or home base before the runner reaches it.
3. An opposing player who has the ball tags him off base.
4. An opponent hits him with a ball when he is off base.

PIN SOCCER

PLAYING FIELD: Playfield or gymnasium.

EQUIPMENT: Soccer ball and four Indian clubs or sticks of wood approximately equal in size.

NUMBER OF PLAYERS: 8–16 players, divided into two teams.

FORMATION: See diagram.

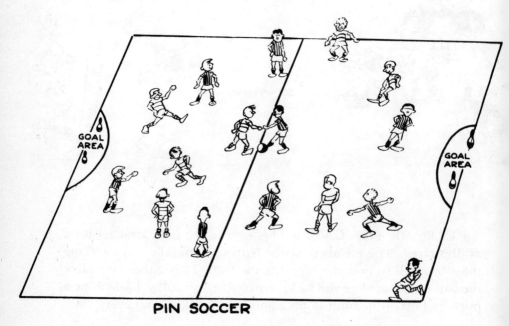

GOAL AREA

GOAL AREA

PIN SOCCER

RULES OF THE GAME: Two pins (Indian clubs) are placed at each end of the field. If the game is to be played outside, the clubs should be fastened to blocks of wood. The players on each team arrange themselves informally within the field. The ball is placed in the center of the field. Two opposing players come to the center; each tries to kick the ball to his teammate. The members of each team attempt to secure the ball. In playing the ball, they may kick, dribble, or pass the ball with their feet, but may not touch it with their hands. Players may not enter the goal area except to retrieve the ball. Two points are scored each time a club is knocked down during play. One point is scored each time a club is knocked down by a free kick. The game is played in 2 halves of 10 minutes each.

The ball is out of bounds when it goes over the sidelines, endlines, or into the goal area. It is thrown in from the place at which it left the field by an opponent of the player who last touched it. No point may be secured on the throw-in. At least 1 other player must play the ball before a point can be scored. The penalty for fouls is a free kick from the center of the field. Opponents may offer no interference or obstruction to a free kick. The fouls are as follows:

1. Touching the ball with the hands.
2. Stepping into the goal area.
3. Pushing, holding, or tripping.

SOCCER PUNT

PLAYING FIELD:	Playfield, soccer field, or football field.
EQUIPMENT:	Soccer ball.
NUMBER OF PLAYERS:	20–40.
FORMATION:	See diagram.

SOCCER PUNT

RULES OF THE GAME: Divide into 2 equal teams. One team starts the game by kicking the ball from a point one third of the distance from their goal line. If a member of the team receiving the ball catches it before it touches the ground, he may take 5 steps toward his opponents' goal and return the kick. The number of steps taken should be adjusted to the group and size of the field. If the ball strikes the ground before it is caught, it must be returned from the spot where is was recovered. A team can not recover its own kick.

Scoring: The team that punts the ball over the goal line scores 1 point. If the ball is caught behind the goal line, the catcher may come out to the goal line and take his 5 steps before returning the kick, and no goal is scored.

After a score, the scored-on team kicks the ball back to its opponents from the kickoff point.

RELAYS

FOOT DRIBBLE RELAY

FORMATION:　　　　　　　See diagram.

RULES OF THE GAME: The head man in each team is given a soccer ball. At a given signal, the first players dribble the ball to the turning line, and then back to the next player. The next player cannot start his dribble until the player ahead has crossed the starting line. The first team to complete its round wins the relay.

Suggestion: As the group progresses, have players use alternate feet and dribble after every 2 or 3 steps. Player should have the ball under control at all times.

SHUTTLE DRIBBLE RELAY

PLAYING FIELD: Playground, gymnasium.

EQUIPMENT: Soccer ball or speedball.

NUMBER OF PLAYERS: 12–40.

SKILLS TO BE TAUGHT: Foot dribble.

FORMATION: See diagram.

RULES OF THE GAME: Divide the players into equal teams and place them in shuttle formation. At a given signal, the first players in A and B teams dribble to the base line, where they pass the ball to the next players. The first team to reach its original position wins the relay.

(*Note:* A player cannot start to dribble until first dribbler has crossed the base line. A player losing control of the ball must recover it and dribble back to the next player. The ball must not be touched with the hands.)

SOCCER PASS RELAY

PLAYING FIELD: Playground or gymnasium.
EQUIPMENT: Soccer ball or speedball.
NUMBER OF PLAYERS: 10–40.
SKILLS TO BE TAUGHT: Inside foot pass, outside foot pass.
FORMATION: See diagram.

SOCCER PASS RELAY

RULES OF THE GAME: Divide the players into equal teams; each team pairs off. At a given signal, the players pass to their partner with an inside or outside pass to the turn line and back to the start line, setting off the next pair. The second pair can not start until the kicking players have crossed the start line. The first team to finish wins the relay.

THROW-IN FOR DISTANCE RELAY

PLAYING FIELD: Playground.
EQUIPMENT: Soccer ball or speedball.
NUMBER OF PLAYERS: 12–40.
FORMATION: See diagram.

RULES OF THE GAME: At a given signal, the first players throw in at the starting line. The second players mark the spot where the balls hit the ground and then throw from that spot. The other players continue the process. The team that has thrown the farthest wins the contest.

ZIGZAG DRIBBLE RELAY

FORMATION: See diagram.

KEEP EYES ON THE BALL

RULES OF THE GAME: Divide the players into equal teams. Place half of the "A" players at the head of the "B" line and half of the "B" players at the head of the "A" line. The other players are spread at 15' intervals.

At a given signal, the first players at the head of "A" and "B" line start to dribble, zigzagging through the line and back to the starting line. The defensive players may kick the ball as it passes in front or behind them. Each defensive player must keep one foot in his original place. When "A" and "B" dribblers finish their dribble, they exchange places with the defensive players and the defensive players become the dribblers. The team that finishes first wins the relay.

BASKETBALL (For Boys)

PLAYING FIELD: Indoor or outdoor basketball court.
EQUIPMENT: Basketball.
NUMBER OF PLAYERS: 10.
FORMATION: See diagram.

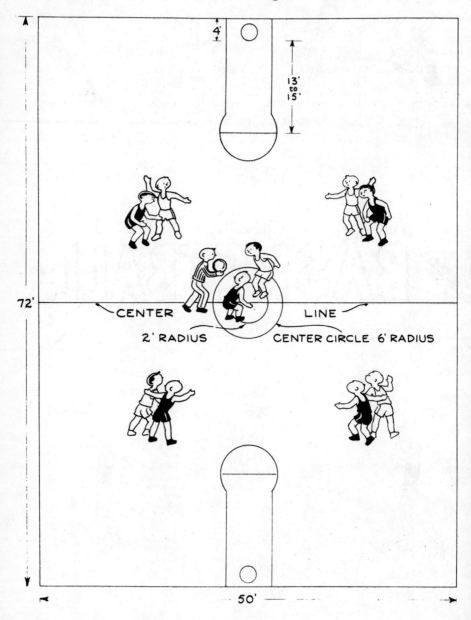

RULES OF THE GAME: Basketball is a game played with 2 teams, each consisting of 5 players, one of whom is captain. The game is started in the center circle by a jump ball. Neither player may tap the ball before it reaches its highest point, and neither may tap the ball more than twice, until after it has touched one of the other 8 players, the floor, the basket, or the backboard. During the center jump, all other players must stay out of the circle. The ball is also put in play in the center circle at the beginning of each quarter and extra period, and after the last free throw following a double foul.

The team with the ball seeks to retain control of it by passing, dribbling, or rolling. It tries to score by shooting the ball through its opponent's basket. The team without the ball seeks to prevent its opponents from shooting the ball into its basket, and at the same time tries to gain possession of the ball.

Game terminology:

A. Back court: the part of the court near the home basket.
   1. A team gaining possession of the ball in its back court must advance it to the front court within 10 seconds unless it is touched by an opponent while it is temporarily out of control, in which case a new 10 second period begins. When the ball is thrown to a team's back court from out of bounds, the 10 seconds count starts as soon as the team has control of the ball. If the 10 second period is exceeded, the opposing team takes the ball out of bounds at the point nearest the violation.
   2. The last person to touch a ball before it goes into the back-court is charged with having caused it to go there. If a player touches the ball before it goes into his own back court, the opposing team takes the ball out of bounds at the point nearest the violation, unless the player sent the ball into his back court after a jump ball, after getting control of the ball from an opponent, or in the course of a "toss-in" from out of bounds.

B. Putting the ball into play after a field goal or foul shot.
   1. Any opponent of the scoring team may put the ball in play from anywhere out of bounds behind the end line, at the end where goal was scored.
   2. On a one-shot foul, if the free throw is made, the ball is taken out of bounds by the opposing team, as above. Under the bonus rule, if both free throws are made, the ball is taken out of bounds in the same manner. The ball is in play if the free throw is missed.

203

C. Putting the ball in play after a held ball or tie ball.
   1. The ball is put into play by a "jump ball" at the restraining circle closest to the spot where the held ball occurred.
   2. Restraining circles: center and free throw circles.

D. Out of bounds.
   1. When a ball goes out of bounds, an official designates the team to throw it in, the ball goes to an opponent of the player who caused it to go out of bounds.
   2. The player taking the ball out of bounds must stand outside the boundary line near the point where the ball left the court, and must throw, bounce, or roll the ball to a player within the court. Five seconds is allowed for this play.

E. Personal fouls.
   1. Kinds:
      a) Holding.
      b) Tripping.
      c) Pushing.
      d) Blocking.
      e) Unnecessary roughness.
      f) Dribbler making personal contact with an opponent, without attempting to avoid it; responsibility for personal contact rests with the dribbler if he tries to dribble by an opponent who is in his path.
   2. Penalties:
      a) If committed on a player who is in the act of shooting for the goal, 2 free throws are awarded if the goal is missed, and 1 if the field goal is made. In the latter case, it counts, and only 1 free throw is awarded.
      b) If the foul is committed under conditions other than those specified in (1), only 1 free throw is awarded. If the foul involves unsportsmanlike conduct, an additional free throw is awarded.
      c) If a double foul is called, only 1 free throw is awarded each team, and play is resumed by a jump ball at center.
      d) Personal fouls are charged to the offender, and a player who commits 5 personal fouls is disqualified.

F. Violations:
   1. Causing the ball to go out of bounds.

204

2. Touching the ball after putting it in play from out of bounds, before it has been touched by another player.
3. Carrying the ball into court from out of bounds.
4. Kicking, punching, or running more than 2 steps with the ball.
5. Completing 1 dribble and then making another one, unless the ball has touched another player, backboard, or basket.
6. Entering the restraining area during the jump ball between other players.
7. Tapping a jump ball before it reaches the highest point or tapping it more than twice before it touches the floor, basket, backboard, or 1 of the other 8 players.
8. Staying in own free throw lane (between end line and free throw line) more than 3 seconds while the ball is in control of a teammate.
9. Using more than 5 seconds to put the ball in play from out of bounds. (For violations A to I inclusive, the ball goes to the opposing team out of bounds.)
10. Touching or crossing the free throw line before the ball touches the ring or backboard, or using more than 10 seconds in making the free throw. In this case the goal does not count and the ball is awarded to the opponent out of bounds at the end boundary line.
11. Touching the free throw line or disconcerting the thrower of a free throw. Penalties:
    a) For a violation by a teammate, the goal does not count and the ball is awarded to the opponents out of bounds at the end line.
    b) For violation by an opponent, the goal counts if made; if missed, another shot is allowed.
    c) For violations by both teams, goal does not count, and play is resumed by a center jump.
12. Interfering with the ball while it is in the opponents' basket. Penalty: the goal is counted whether made or not, and play is resumed as after a field goal.

G. Substitutions.
    1. A substitute must report to the scorer, giving his name, number, and position before going on the court.
    2. A substitute must remain outside the boundary line until an official signals for him to enter the court.

H. Time out.
1. Is called by the official when:
    a) A foul is called.
    b) He suspends play because of injury to a player.
    c) He grants a player's request for time out, such request being granted only when the ball is dead or in control of the player's team.
    d) There is a delay in obtaining the ball.
2. Five time-outs allowed each team without penalty.

I. Playing periods.
1. Four quarters of 6 minutes each, with a 2-minute rest period between quarters and a 10-minute rest period between halves.
2. If the score is tied at the end of the regular playing period, the game continues after a 5-minute rest period, and the first team to score 2 points wins the game.

J. Miscellaneous terms.
1. Disqualified player: one who commits 5 personal fouls or certain flagrant fouls, and is barred from further participation in the game.
2. Double foul: simultaneous fouling of two opponents by each other.
3. Dribble: throwing, batting, or bouncing the ball in such a manner that it contacts the floor, and is touched by the player again before being touched by another player. A player may begin a dribble by tossing the ball into the air, and touching it again before it touches the floor. The dribble is complete the instant the player touches the ball simultaneously with both hands or permits the ball to come to rest in one or both hands. A player may take as many steps as he wishes between bounces of the dribble.
4. Foul: any infraction of the rules, for which the penalty is one or more free throws.
    a) Personal fouls.
    b) Technical fouls.
5. Jump ball: the official tosses the ball up between two opposing players.
6. Multiple throw: a succession of free throws attempted by the same team.
7. Pivot: a circular movement by a player, who is holding the

ball, in stepping once or more than once in any direction with the same foot, the other foot remaining in place.

8. Violation: any infraction of the rules not involving a foul.
9. Blocking: personal contact which impedes the progress of an opponent who does not have the ball.
10. Dead ball: play ceases:
    a) When goal is made.
    b) When time out is declared.
    c) When foul or violations are called.
    d) After each free throw, and following a technical or double foul.
    e) When the ball goes out of bounds.
    f) When a held ball is declared.
    g) After each free throw of a multiple throw, except when the last throw was awarded for a personal foul and is unsuccessful.
    h) When the ball lodges in the supports of the basket.
    i) At the expiration of playing time.
    j) When the whistle of an official sounds.
11. Free throw: an attempt to score one point by an unhindered throw from the free throw line.
12. Front and back court: the front court is that part of the court between the offensive team's end line and the nearer edge of the division line. The back court is the other part of the court, including the division line.
13. Held ball: a held ball is declared when 2 players of opposing teams have one or both hands firmly on the ball, or when a closely guarded player who is in his front court is making no effort to put the ball in play.
14. Holding: personal contact which interferes with the freedom of movement of an opponent. ("Guarding from the rear" which results in personal contact is a personal foul.)
15. Out of bounds:
    a) The ball is out of bounds when it touches the floor or any person or object on or outside a boundary line or the supports of the backboards.
    b) A player is out of bounds when he touches the floor on or outside the boundary lines.
16. Running with the ball (traveling): progressing in any direction in excess of the following limits while holding the ball:

a) A player may pivot on either foot if he receives the ball while standing.

b) A player is allowed a two-count rhythm in coming to a stop or getting rid of the ball at the completion of a dribble, or if he is moving when he receives the ball.

c) If the player comes to a stop on the count of 1, he may pivot and may use either foot as the pivot foot.

d) If the player comes to a stop on the count of 2, and one foot is in advance of the other, he may lift either foot, provided he gets rid of the ball before that foot again touches the floor; but if one foot is in advance of the other, he may pivot on the rear foot only.

K. Scoring.
1. Field goal: two points.
2. Free throw: one point.

BASKETBALL TECHNIQUE

I. Two-hand foul shot: in the modern game of basketball, foul shooting has become a deciding factor in a close, hard fought game, and games are often won or lost at the foul line.

A. Stance.
1. The toe of the forward foot should be placed about one inch back from the foul line.
2. Players may place their feet parallel behind the free throw line with feet spread comfortably.

B. Holding the ball.
  1. Hold the ball at the waist or downward at the full length of the arms; the hands should be slightly back of the center of the ball.
  2. The fingers should be spread evenly and comfortably on the side of the ball.
     a) The heel of the hand should be off the ball.
     b) The fingers should be pointed down.
     c) Thumbs should point toward the basket.
C. Shooting action.
  1. Eyes should be on the forward rim of the basket.
  2. Take a deep breath; hold for a second to help steady nerves.
  3. Start the throwing motion.
     a) Bend knees to a comfortable crouch.
     b) Keep arms straight.
     c) Keep body weight slightly forward on the balls of the feet.
     d) Drop the ball between the knees.
     e) Come up out of the crouch position; the arms make an arc with a free and natural upward motion, releasing the ball at about eye level.
     f) Do not attempt to put on a backspin with wrist action.
D. Follow-through.
  1. Keep eyes on the rim of the basket until the shot reaches the rim.
  2. Keep perfect body balance, with the weight of body forward on the toes.
  3. The palms of the hands should be facing inward and forward toward the basket about 10″ to 12″ apart.

II. Ball receiving.
  A. Keep eyes on the ball, body relaxed and ready.
  B. Hands should be advanced, elbows in; the fingers should be well spread, with the thumbs in.
  C. The ball should meet the tip of the fingers first; arms and shoulders should be relaxed and held slightly toward the body to absorb the speed of the ball.
  D. Player should move to meet the ball; this prevents interceptions.

III. The chest pass: hand position is the most important funda-
mental to learn in ball handling.
   A. Position of hands on the ball; see diagram.
      1. Both hands on ball, fingers slightly spread a little above
         and behind the center of the ball.
      2. Never let the palms of the hand touch the ball; let the
         fingers control the ball.
   B. Body position in passing; see diagram.
      1. Body bent slightly forward at waist, head up.
      2. Feet, legs, and body in a balanced position.

C. Arm position: elbows bent and held slightly away from the body. Follow-through ball release; see diagram.
   1. Drop hands slightly and extend the arms with a snap through with the wrists and fingers.
   2. To make your follow-through a smooth action and your pass soft and easily handled, step out with your pass on either foot, shifting the weight of the body to the forward foot.
      a) You are in position to follow pass or break for a return pass.
      b) Just push your pass: don't try to put on reverse action with too much wrist action.

IV. Stopping: The two-count is usually used when a man is dribbling and is stopped by the approach of a defensive man.
   A. Position of two-count stop; either foot may be ahead.
      1. Knees and hips should be flexed, center of gravity low, and the body bent forward.
      2. Feet should be well spread, weight on forward foot, and elbows in close to the body.
      3. On a count or stride stop, the rear foot is always the pivot foot, unless the second foot comes down parallel with the first foot, in which case, either foot may be the pivot foot.

B. Position of one-count stop: player comes to a stop with both feet hitting the floor simultaneously.
   1. Player should have his feet in a wide base, shoulder width apart, knees flexed and elbows close to body.
   2. Back should be straight and head up.
   3. Ball should be held firmly in both hands about waist high.
   4. The center of gravity should be low, body and feet in a position to pivot in any direction.

V. The pivot: usually used after a dribble stop to maneuver away from a defensive man.
   A. The reverse pivot. Either foot may be used as the pivot foot.
      1. Shift weight to pivot foot and shove off with opposite foot.
      2. Player may swing around in a complete circle in either direction, or as much of the circle as he wishes as long as the pivot foot contacts the floor.
      3. Reverse pivot from a one-two count stop or stride stop: pivot must be made on the rear foot.

   B. Body actions.
      1. The body is in a crouched position.
      2. The ball is held low out from the body and kept moving.
      3. Head is up, eyes on the field, looking for a teammate maneuver.
      4. Pivot should be made away from a guard.
      5. Pivoter should be able to pivot equally well in either direction.

VI. The defensive stance: is an important factor in defensive play. The offensive player knows what he is going to do, but since the guard does not know his intended action or direction, he must be in a stance that will give him the greatest mobility. A defensive player must be alert and ready to move in any direction.

A. Parallel stance.
  1. Feet: should be spread comfortably (about shoulder width), with the weight evenly divided on the balls of the feet.
  2. Knees: should be flexed.
  3. Back: straight.
  4. Arms: bent at the elbows or spread wide, with hands in position to meet the play.
    a) Raise the hands to stop overhead shots or passes.
    b) Lower hands to block low or bounce passes.
  5. Head: up.
  6. Foot work: use boxers' style in shifting the feet.
    a) Use short quick shuffle steps in maneuvering.
    b) Do not cross the feet.
    c) A guard must not get too close to an offensive man who is a quick starter or a good faker.

VII. The dribble; the act of giving impetus to the ball by batting or bouncing, thus advancing the ball. The player may take as many steps as he wishes between the bounces of the ball. The hands may be used alternately for each dribble, or the right or the left may be used alone.

A. Position.

    1. Body:

        a) Back straight, with the weight of the body forward.

        b) Knees bent, hips dropped, body relaxed.

        c) Head up, eyes ahead.

2. Arms and hands:
   a) Rotate the right hand on top of the ball, left hand under the ball, in the starting position of the dribble. (For right hand dribbler.)
   b) The active forearm should be parallel with the floor; free arm should be away from side.
   c) The wrists and fingers should be relaxed, with the fingers cupped for better control.
B. Action.
   1. The ball should be touched with the fingertips, not with the palm of the hand.

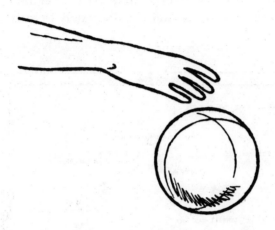

   2. The ball should be kept ahead of the feet far enough to avoid contact with the dribbler's body, but not so far ahead that control becomes difficult.
   3. The forearms should move upward about 5 inches and downward about 10 inches from the parallel line of position.
C. Uses.
   1. Advancing the ball.
   2. Keeping possession of the ball.
   3. Faking opponents out of position.
D. Coaching suggestions.
   1. Player should not slap the ball.
   2. Player should be able to divide his attention between the ball and the general playing situation.
   3. Dribble should be used only when a pass is not possible.

SIMPLIFIED BASKETBALL FOR GIRLS

Girls' basketball is essentially the same as the regular game. The few differences are as follows:

1. There are 6 players on each team: 3 forwards and 3 guards.
2. The court is divided into halves: one half for forwards, and the other for guards. The guards may not cross into the forwards' area, and vice versa.
3. The game consists of four 5-minute quarters, with 5-minute rest periods between quarters, and a 10-minute rest period at the half.
4. The referee begins the game by throwing the ball to a center, who has been previously determined by flipping a coin. Only the centers may occupy the 6-foot center circle. At the beginning of each quarter, the center throw is awarded alternately to each team.

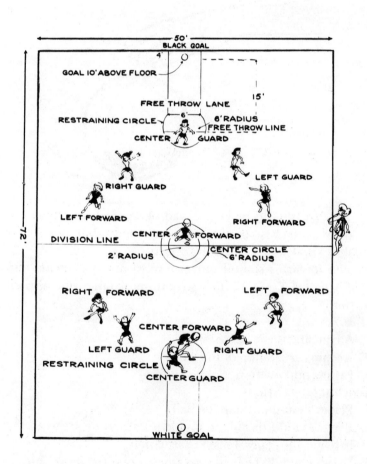

5. Violations: ball is put into play from out of bounds by the team opposite the offending player's.
   a) Kicking the ball intentionally.
   b) Striking the ball with the fist.
   c) Handing the ball to another player.
   d) Stepping over the half-court line.
6. Terminology:
   a) Bouncing: ball is bounced and caught as a player advances; a player is allowed 2 bounces in succession.
   b) Limited dribble: player gives impetus to the ball twice, causing it to bounce at least 2 times, and then touches or regains possession of it.
   c) Tie ball: two players of opposing teams place one or both hands firmly on the ball at the same time.

Questions regarding additional rules may be answered by referring to the Official Basketball Guide, published for the National Section for Girls and Women Sports by the American Assoc. for Health and Physical Education and Recreation, 1201 Sixteenth St., N.W., Washington 6, D.C.

DRILLS

BASKETBALL DRIBBLE AND PIVOT

PLAYING FIELD:	Gymnasium, playground, or playroom.
EQUIPMENT:	Two basketballs.
NUMBER OF PLAYERS:	30–60.
FORMATION:	See diagram.

RULES OF THE GAME: Divide players into 2 or more teams, and mark a line 60'–70' from the starting point. The first man on each team has a basketball, and on a whistle, each starts dribbling to the end line. On the whistle, each player stops and makes a reverse pivot and stands facing the opposite direction until the leader whistles again. Then, with another reverse pivot, he dribbles until the next whistle.

When a player finally gets to the end line, he must dribble around the end line and dribble back toward his team. On getting back to his team, he hands the ball to the next player. The game continues until all have competed, or until the first team finishing is declared the winning team.

CIRCLE SHOOTING DRILL

PLAYING FIELD:
Gymnasium or playground with baskets.

EQUIPMENT:
Basketballs.

NUMBER OF PLAYERS:
10–20.

FORMATION:
See diagram.

RULES OF THE GAME:
The players form a circle around the basket. Each takes the type of shot the leader calls. After all players have shot, they rotate one place counter-clockwise. The leader then calls for another type of shot, etc.

DRIBBLE, LAY-UP, AND REBOUND DRILL

PLAYING FIELD: Gymnasium or playground with baskets.

EQUIPMENT: Basketballs.

NUMBER OF PLAYERS: 10–30.

A.   **DRIBBLE, LAY-UP,**   **B.**
AND REBOUND DRILL

RULES OF THE GAME: Assign 10 players to a basket. The first player stands under the basket with the ball, while the other players form a line at a distance from the basket. The first player in the line runs toward the basket, receives a pass from the waiting player, dribbles and shoots at the basket. He recovers the ball and passes to the next player in the line, while the player who passed to him goes to the end of the line.

DRIBBLE PASS

PLAYING FIELD: Gymnasium or playground with baskets.

EQUIPMENT: Basketballs.

NUMBER OF PLAYERS: 10–40.

FORMATION: See diagram.

RULES OF THE GAME: Divide the players into 4 or more teams and divide each team, placing each half at a pass line. Give the balls to the first players. At a given signal, the number one players dribble the ball to the opposite pass line and pass the balls to the number two players, who in turn dribble back to the opposite pass line. After the ball is passed to each succeeding player, the passer goes to the end of the line.

Variations: Left hand dribble. Alternate hand dribble. Stop on a whistle and start ahead again on a whistle.

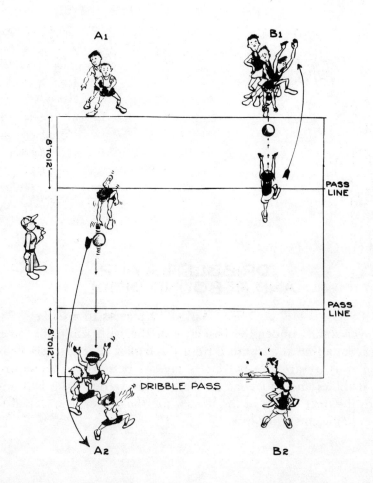

FIVE ROUNDS

PLAYING FIELD:
Gymnasium, playfield, or playroom.

EQUIPMENT:
Basketball, volleyball, or soccer ball.

NUMBER OF PLAYERS:
12–40, divided into equal teams of 6, 8, or 10.

FORMATION:
See diagram.

RULES OF THE GAME:
Give the captain of each team a ball. At a given signal, the ball is passed from one player to the next around the circle in a prescribed manner (to the right, left, underhanded pass, two-handed pass, overhead pass, bounce pass). Each time the ball returns to the captain, he calls out, "One!" "Two!" etc. At the completion of the fifth round the captain holds the ball above his head. Each player must handle the ball on every round in the prescribed manner. The team to complete the 5 rounds first is the winner.

In a soccer drill, the ball is kicked with the right or left foot.

20' TO 40'

MEET-THE-BALL-AND-PASS DRILL

PLAYING FIELD:	Gymnasium or playground.
EQUIPMENT:	Basketballs.
NUMBER OF PLAYERS:	10–12 per basket.
FORMATION:	See diagram.

RULES OF THE GAME: The players form 2 lines, which stand about 20 feet from each other. The first player in the "A" line passes

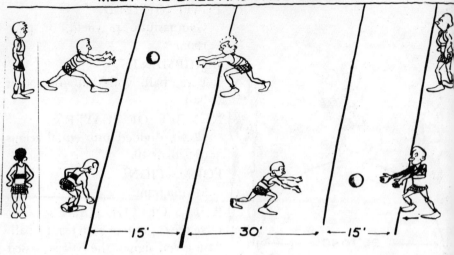

the ball to the first player in the "B" line; the latter should run toward the ball to receive the pass. After each pass, the players go to the ends of the opposite lines.

1-2 STOP!

WHEN COACH BLOWS WHISTLE
PLAYERS COME TO <u>ONE</u>, <u>TWO</u>, <u>STOP</u>.

STOP DRILL

PLAYING FIELD:
Gymnasium, playroom, or playfield.

EQUIPMENT:
Basketballs.

NUMBER OF PLAYERS:
6–40.

FORMATION:
See diagram.

RULES OF THE DRILL:
Players leave the starting line on the whistle and come to a 1–2 stop on the whistle. Purpose: To practice stopping without taking more than the 1–2 count.

222

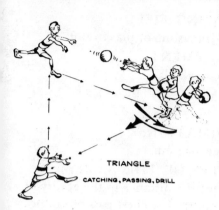

TRIANGLE
CATCHING, PASSING, DRILL

PLAYING FIELD:
  Gymnasium or playground.

EQUIPMENT:
  Basketballs.

NUMBER OF PLAYERS:
  Groups of 3.

FORMATION:
  See diagram.

RULES OF THE GAME:
  Practice the chest pass, bounce pass, fake and pass.

ZIGZAG DRIBBLE DRILL

PLAYING FIELD:
  Gymnasium, playroom, or playground.

EQUIPMENT:
  Basketballs.

NUMBER OF PLAYERS:
  6–40.

FORMATION:
  See diagram.

RULES OF THE GAME:
Number one player starts dribbling in and out between the players in the line, back to his original position, and passes the ball to number two player. Number two dribbles in and out between the players, around number one, back to his original position, and passes the ball to number three player.

Variation: Dribble left handed; alternate dribble hands.

ZIGZAG PASSING AND CATCHING DRILL

PLAYING FIELD:
  Gymnasium or playground.
EQUIPMENT:
  Basketballs.
NUMBER OF PLAYERS:
  6–40.
FORMATION:
  See diagram.
RULES OF THE GAME:
Adjust the distance to the ability of the group. Use chest pass or bounce pass. Make passes short and snappy.
  Hints: Step with the pass. Use the elbows as the shock absorber.

PASSING, CATCHING, DRILL

LEAD-UP GAMES

NINE-COURT BASKETBALL

PLAYING FIELD: Basketball court, divided into 9 equal areas.

EQUIPMENT: Basketball, volleyball, or soccer ball.

NUMBER OF PLAYERS: 2 teams of 9 players each.

FORMATION: See diagram.

RULES OF THE GAME: Each player has an area within which he must stay. Only the forwards may shoot baskets, which count 2 points each. The game begins with a toss-up at center or a throw-in from the sideline, as in regular basketball for girls. After the toss-up or throw-in, each team attempts to get the ball to their forwards so they can score. Players may not take more than one step with the ball, or step over a boundary line. They may dribble once, girls using 2 hands. Infraction of a rule or causing the ball to go out-of-bounds gives the ball to the opponents at the spot where the infraction occurred.

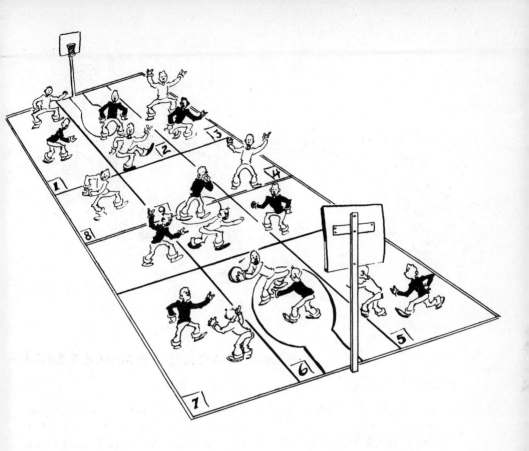

NINE-COURT
BASKETBALL

Touching the ball when an opponent has it in his possession, any body contact, or other unfair act, is a foul. The penalty for a foul is one free shot unguarded, which counts 1 point if made.

ONE-BASKET BASKETBALL

PLAYING FIELD:	One half of a basketball court, or space where one basket is available.
EQUIPMENT:	Basket and basketball.
NUMBER OF PLAYERS:	4 to 10 per team.
FORMATION:	See diagram.

40'TO45'

40'

ONE-BASKET BASKETBALL

RULES OF THE GAME: Basketball rules are used, with this exception. The team having possession of the ball may shoot for a basket. If the opposing team gains possession of the ball, they must take the ball back past the foul line before they can attempt a basket. If a player on the team that attempted the goal recovers the ball, he may shoot for the basket again without bringing it out over the foul line.

SOFTBALL

PLAYING FIELD:
EQUIPMENT:

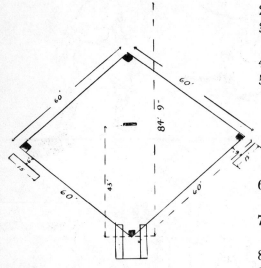

PITCHERS PLATE

Softball diamond: see diagram.

1. Home plate made of hard rubber, set flush with the ground.
2. Three bases 15″ square.
3. Rubber or wood pitcher's plate 2′ x 6″ set flush with ground.
4. Bats, regulation type.
5. Softballs: leather, smooth seamed or rubber, rubber covered, and containing yarn and kapok; diameter not less than 11-7/8″ or more than 12-1/8″; 6 to 8 ounces in weight.
6. Gloves may be worn by any player.
7. Mitts, limited to first baseman and catcher.
8. Masks, worn by catcher.
9. Spikes, or any other sharp projection, prohibited.
10. Cleats, if worn, must be of hard rubber extending not more than 3/8″ from sole of shoe.
11. Catcher's chest protector, required for girls, optional for boys.

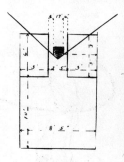

BASE RUNNING
NO LEAD OFF OF BASE

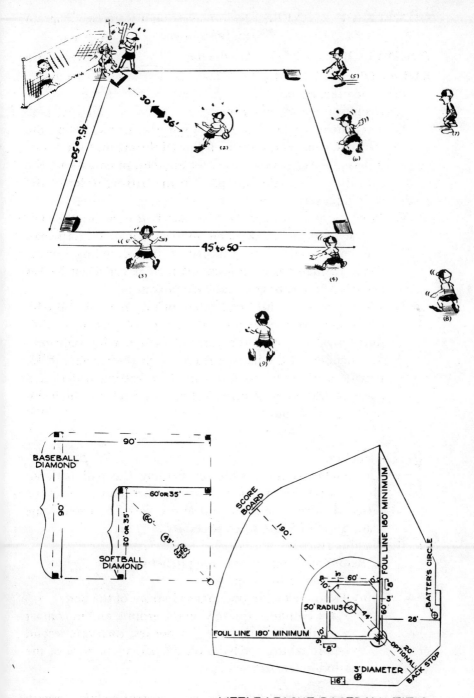

30'
36'

45' to 50'

45' to 50'

(2)

(3)

(4)

(5)

(6)

(7)

(8)

(9)

90'

BASEBALL
DIAMOND

90'

60' OR 35'

60' OR 35'

60'

45'

60°

SOFTBALL
DIAMOND

SCORE
BOARD

FOUL LINE 180' MINIMUM

190'

60'

FOUL LINE 180' MINIMUM

50' RADIUS

44'

60'

28'

3'

20'

OPTIONAL

BATTER'S CIRCLE

3' DIAMETER

BACK STOP

8'

8'

16'

LITTLE LEAGUE BASEBALL FIELD

NUMBER OF PLAYERS: Nine players on a team (see diagram for positions).

FORMATION: See diagram.

RULES OF THE GAME:*

I. Pregame preparation.
   A. Decide on the batting team.
   B. The batting order of each team must be formed before the start of a game and must be followed throughout the game, unless a player is substituted for another, in which case the substitute must take the place in the batting order of the retired player.
   C. After the first inning, the first batter in each inning shall be the batsman whose name follows that of the last man who completed his turn at bat in the preceding inning. (The batsman has completed his turn at bat when he has become a base runner or has been put out.)
   D. When playing an informal game such as in a physical education class or on a picnic, the players of each team may number off or bat in the order of their playing positions.
   E. All members of the batting team except the batsman must remain behind the backstop in their batting order; if a batsman leaves his position behind the backstop his team shall receive an out.

II. The pitcher.
   A. The pitcher is responsible for fielding the ball between pitcher's plate and home, fielding short bunts down the first and third base lines, and also covers first base, home plate, and third base when necessary.
   B. Pitching rules.
      1. Before pitching the ball, the pitcher shall:
         a) Come to a full stop.
         b) Hold the ball in both hands in front of the body.
         c) Have both feet squarely on the ground and in contact with the pitcher's plate, for not less than one second before taking one hand off the ball at the start of the wind-up or back-swing.

* Women's Official Softball Guide: National Section on Women's Athletics. American Assn. for Health, Physical Ed., and Recreation (1201 Sixteenth St., N.W., Washington 6, D.C.). Official Softball Guide: New York: A. S. Barnes and Co.

d) Not be considered in pitching position unless the catcher is in position to receive the pitch.

e) Take but one step forward while in the act of delivering the ball; the step must be taken simultaneously with the delivery of the ball to the batsman.

f) Must not hold the ball more than 20 seconds before pitching it to the batter.

2. For a legal delivery, the ball must be thrown underhanded with hand and wrist following through past the straight line of the body before the ball is released.

3. The pitcher may use any wind-up he desires, provided that in the final delivery of the ball to the batter, his hand shall be below the hip, and the wrist not farther from the body than the elbow.

III. The batter.
   A. Goes to first base when:
      1. Ball is hit into fair territory and he reaches the base safely.
      2. He is walked (receives 4 balls).
      3. The pitched ball, not struck at, touches any part of the batsman while he is standing in the batting position, unless, in the opinion of the umpire, he makes no effort to get out of the way of the pitched ball.
   B. Is out when:
      1. He has 3 strikes.
      2. He hits a fair or foul ball that is caught by a fielder.
      3. He is tagged before reaching first base.
      4. A foul tip on the third strike is caught by the catcher.
      5. He bunts the ball foul on the third strike.
      6. He bats out of order.
      7. He attempts to hinder the catcher from fielding or throwing the ball by stepping outside the lines of the batsman's position.
      8. First base is touched by a player with the ball before the the batter reaches the base.

IV. Base advances.
   A. When forced by another runner.
   B. After a fly ball has been caught.
   C. After the ball has left the pitcher's hand.

D. On any fair hit ball that is not caught.

E. On an overthrow or passed ball (at his own risk).

V. Base runner is out after:

A. A fly ball is caught, and the fielder throws the ball to a teammate on the base before the runner retouches the base. The runner may leave the base as soon as the fly ball hits the fielder's glove.

B. Being tagged by a fielder with the ball in his possession if the runner is off base when tagged.

C. He leaves the base before the ball leaves the pitcher's hand.

D. He is forced out by another runner. (The fielder with the ball in his possession tags the base before the runner reaches the base.)

E. He runs more than 3 feet out from the base line to avoid being touched, except when a fielder is fielding a ball in the base runner's path.

F. He obstructs or intentionally interferes with a fielder in attempting to field a batted ball or recovering a ball.

G. Advancing bases and failing to touch a base. The fielder with the ball in his possession may tag the base before he returns or tag the runner with the ball.

H. He passes a preceding base runner before such a runner has been legally put out.

VI. Scoring.

A. One run is scored every time a base runner, after having legally touched the first 3 bases, legally touches the home base before 3 men are put out. If a player reaches home on or during a play in which the third man is forced out or is put out before reaching first base, the run shall not count; also, if the third out is made by a preceding runner failing to touch a base, the run shall not count.

B. No run shall be scored on any play in which the third man is called out for leaving the base before a pitched ball has left the pitcher's hand.

VII. After three outs:

A. The batting team goes to the field, and the fielding team goes to bat.

B. An inning is completed after both teams have had three outs.

C. Seven innings constitute a game.

VIII. A legally batted fair ball:
   A. Settles in fair ground between home and first base, or between home and third base.
   B. Is on or over fair territory when bounding to the outfield.
   C. Touches first base or third base.
   D. First falls in fair territory beyond first and third base.
   E. Must be judged as such according to the relative position of the ball and the foul line, and not in relation to the fielder and his position on the ground at the time he touches the ball.

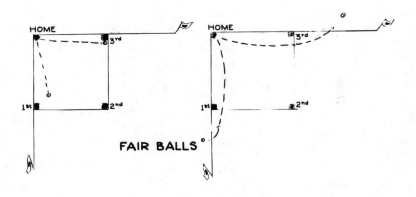

FAIR BALLS

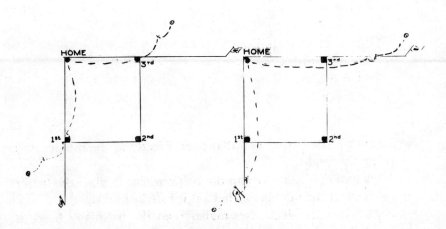

IX. A legally batted foul ball:
   A. Settles in foul territory between home and first base, or between home and third base.
   B. Bounds past first or third base on or over foul territory.
   C. Falls in foul territory beyond first or third base.
   D. Touches any person or object, such as a bat, glove, fence, bench, or screen, or is handled by a fielder while on or over foul territory; a ball thus interfered with is a foul ball regardless of where it may go thereafter.

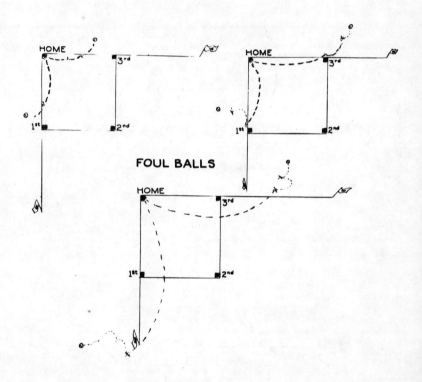

FOUL BALLS

X. A foul tip is a batted ball that goes directly to the catcher and is legally caught.
   A. A foul tip is a strike and the ball remains in play; the batter is out if the catcher catches a third strike foul tip.
   B. A foul ball which rises higher than the batsman's head, is not called a foul tip, but is a foul ball.

BASIC FUNDAMENTAL SKILLS AND
TECHNIQUES FOR SOFTBALL

I. Overhand throw. (For right-handed players.)
  A. Position.
    1. First two fingers of the right hand on top of the ball, thumb on inside, third and fourth finger on the outside.

  B. Action.
    1. The hand is brought back with a swing well behind and a little above the shoulder.
    2. The left side of the body is turned in the direction of the throw.
    3. The left arm is raised and carried around the front of the body below shoulder height.
    4. Left foot is forward, toe touching the ground.
    5. Place the weight on the right foot.
    6. The throw is made with a downward snap of the wrist, adding speed to the arm movement.
    7. As the arm moves forward, the body follows through, putting the weight of the body into the throw. At the conclusion of the throw, the right foot is pointing in the direction of the throw.

II. Underhand throw.
A. Position.
1. Pitcher stands facing home plate with both feet slightly apart on the pitcher's plate, holding the ball in front of the body with both hands.

B. Action.
1. On the back swing of the arm (pendulum swing), the ball is held in the right hand with the palm down, elbow slightly flexed.
2. The body twists to the right on the back swing and a left-foot step is taken in the direction of the throw.
3. On the follow-through, the throwing hand is palm up about chest high, the right foot comes to a stride position parallel with the left foot, and the knees are slightly flexed so that the pitcher is in position to field a ball.

III. Fielding grounders.
   A. Position: the fielder's feet are spread comfortably and parallel, knees slightly bent, and the weight on the balls of the feet.
   B. Action.
      1. Play the ball: run in to field a ground ball; do not wait for it or back up.
      2. Keep your eyes on the ball: follow it into your glove.
      3. Hands should be in front of the body, left foot slightly advanced, and the glove close to the ground; keep the head down.
      4. After fielding the ball, bring the arm back to the throwing position in a quick smooth motion; step with your left foot and throw with right hand.

IV. Catching, above the waist.
   A. Position.
      1. The feet are in a walking position, the left foot forward, weight evenly distributed.
   B. Action.
      1. Hands up, arms extended, palms facing oncoming ball.
      2. Fingers pointed up, cupped with the thumbs together.
      3. As the ball drops into the hands, the hands should be pulled back to break the impact.
      4. Learn to judge the spot at which a fly ball will come down.
      5. Avoid backing up to make a catch. Turn and run to the spot where the ball is expected to drop, glancing over the shoulder while running.

V. Catching, below the waist.
   A. Position.
      1. The feet are in a walking position, weight evenly distributed, body bent slightly forward.
      2. Hands and arms are extended, with the little fingers held together.
   B. Action.
      1. Hands and arms are in position to make the catch.
      2. Turn cupped palms toward the ball, fingers pointing down.

3. At the impact of the ball, let the hands and arms go rearward with the ball's impetus.

VI. Batting.
   A. Position.
      1. Stand with feet spread comfortably and elbows away from the body to allow freedom for the swing; keep shoulders and hips level; right-handed batters turn the left side toward the pitcher; while left-handed batters turn the right side toward the pitcher.
      2. Have the trade mark on the bat up; hold the bat at or above the shoulder, but do not rest the bat on the shoulder; grip the bat with both hands close together. The right-handed batter has his right hand nearest the end of the bat, the left, vice versa.
      3. Keep relaxed until just before the ball is thrown; have eyes on the pitcher and be ready for the pitch; do not keep swinging the bat back and forth when the pitcher is ready to deliver the ball.
   B. Action.
      1. As the pitcher releases the ball, keep eyes on the ball.
      2. Take a short 6″–10″ slide step toward the pitcher, but have the foot set before swinging the bat.
      3. As the bat is swung to meet the ball, tighten the grip on the bat just before the ball is hit, and swing the bat parallel to the ground.
         a) The weight of the body shifts from the rear foot to the front foot.

b) The wrist action comes as the ball is hit.

c) The ball is hit out in front of the plate.

4. The bat and arms follow through in an arc as the body twists to the left, using the front foot as the pivot point (opposite for a left-handed batter).

5. Be in a position to run to first base quickly.

6. Drop the bat; DON'T THROW IT!

VII. Bunting.

A. Position: feet remain as in regular closed batting stance.

B. The bunt: a bunt is a batted ball which is tapped slowly within the infield.

BATTING AND BASE RUNNING DRILLS

PLAYING FIELD: Softball diamond.

EQUIPMENT: Batting tee, softballs, bases, and bats.

NUMBER OF PLAYERS: 10–30. Over 15 players form another game.

FORMATION: See diagram.

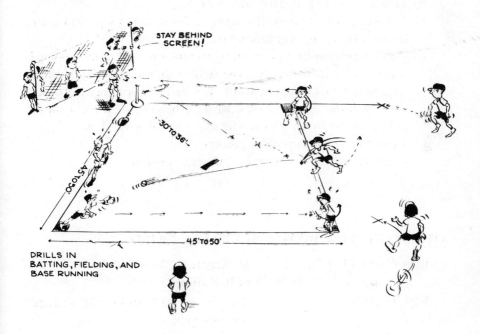

DRILLS IN BATTING, FIELDING, AND BASE RUNNING

RULES OF THE GAME:

1. The batter hits 3 balls off the tee.

   a) All balls fielded in the infield are thrown to first base, first base throws to second, and second to third. Third throws home and the catcher places the ball on the tee.

   b) Balls fielded in left and center field are thrown into second base and then to first, back to second, third, and home.

   c) Balls hit into right field are thrown directly to first base and then around the bases.

   d) On the batter's third hit, he tries to beat the ball around the bases. The run may be timed if a stop watch is available.

241

e) After the batter has rounded the bases, he goes to right field, and the other players rotate one position, the catcher going to bat.

f) If there are more than 10 players, the extras wait their turn at bat behind the backstop.

g) The practice drill is ended when all players have had a turn at batting.

2. Skills to teach:

a) Better batting position.

b) Quick starts to first base; base-touching.

c) Infielding on all bases: throwing in from fielder's position, and quick relay of the ball around the bases.

d) Fielder getting into position to receive the ball as soon as it is hit; on a hard hit fly ball, the fielder should practice running toward the spot where he thinks the ball can be caught. Toward the end of the run, he should turn his head to keep a line on the ball, in order to judge when he should turn to catch it.

e) Learning to back-up other players.

f) Gaining skill in throwing in different positions.

OVERHAND THROW FOR ACCURACY DRILLS

PLAYING FIELD: Gymnasium, handball court, or side of building.

EQUIPMENT: Target on wall, three 12″ softballs for each group.

NUMBER OF PLAYERS: 10–40.

FORMATION: See diagram.

RULES OF THE GAME: Divide the group into squads of 6–8 players.

1. Number one man on each team throws at the target.
2. Each member of the squad makes 3 successive throws at the target.
3. After the third throw, all players rotate as diagramed.
4. A round is over when all players have thrown at the target from a specified distance.

a) First round......25′

b) Second round....35′

c) Third round.....45′

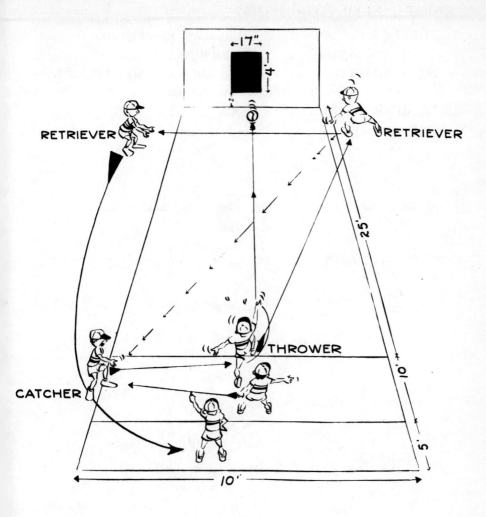

5. Scoring:
   a) The player who follows the thrower will be his scorekeeper for
      each game.
   b) At the end of the game, the player with the most points is de-
      clared the winner.
   c) When there is more than one team, scoring may be placed on a
      team basis, and the team receiving the highest score wins.

Variation: This drill may be used with a 10″ ball.

UNDERHANDED PITCH DRILL

PLAYING FIELD:	Gymnasium, handball court, or side of a building.
EQUIPMENT:	Target on wall, three 12″ softballs for each group.
NUMBER OF PLAYERS:	10–40.
FORMATION:	See diagram.

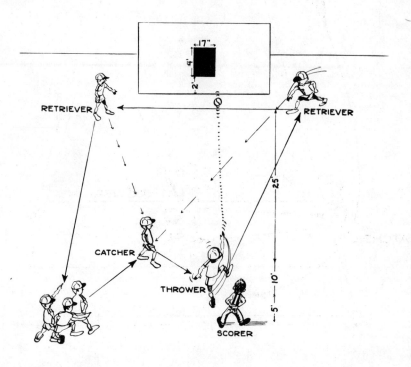

RULES OF THE GAME: Divide the group into squads of 6–8 players.

1. The thrower stands on the pitcher's plate, 25′ from the target, and throws 6 times. The player standing behind the thrower scores the hits.
2. Rotation: the thrower becomes the right retriever, then the left retriever, then the catcher, and finally returns to the line.
3. This procedure is repeated until all players have had a turn.
4. The second round is thrown from 35′, the third round from 40′.
5. This game can be played as an individual or a team competition.

ZIGZAG THROW AND CATCH DRILLS

PLAYING FIELD: Gymnasium, playfield, or playroom.
EQUIPMENT: Softballs.
NUMBER OF PLAYERS: 10–40.
FORMATION: See diagram.

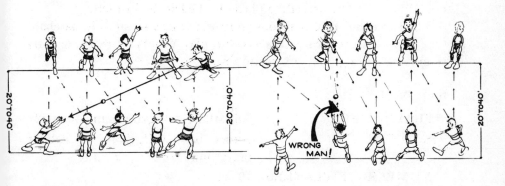

RULES OF THE DRILL: Divide the group into squads of 6–8 players. Practice skills in:
1. Throwing: underhand and overhand.
2. Catching: slow and fast balls, grounders, and fly balls.

LEAD-UP GAMES

BAR KICK BASEBALL

PLAYING FIELD: Softball or smaller diamond.
EQUIPMENT: Paper bar, rolled and tied tightly (newspaper will do nicely), and 2 blocks across which the paper is laid.
NUMBER OF PLAYERS: 3 to 12 per team.
FORMATION: See diagram.

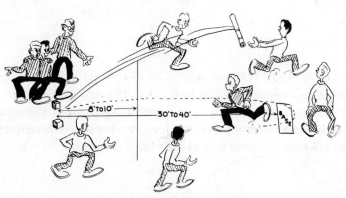

RULES OF THE GAME: The blocks and bar are set up at home plate. The batter kicks the bar as far as he can, then runs the bases. The team in the field spreads out in front of the line and attempts to replace the bar while the runner is off base. A foul ball is one kicked outside the field of play, or one that fails to cross the scratch line, which is 10′ from the plate. A foul ball puts the batter out and returns the preceding player to the base he just left.

The two teams take positions and rotate turns at bat as in baseball. One point is scored for each successful play; 3 outs retire a side. Any number of innings may constitute a game.

BAT BALL

PLAYING FIELD:	Softball field or gymnasium 40′ x 72′.
EQUIPMENT:	Soccer ball, volleyball, or rubber playground ball.
NUMBER OF PLAYERS:	10–24.
FORMATION:	See diagram.

RULES OF THE GAME: The team scatters in the field. The batter stands on the serving line, tosses the ball into the air, and bats with his hand or fist. The ball must be hit beyond the scratch line, which is 10 feet from the serving line. After a successful hit, the batter runs to the base, circles it, and runs back to home.

The fielders field the ball and attempt to hit the runner with it. A fielder can not take more than 2 steps with the ball. He must pass the ball to his teammates in an attempt to strike the base runner. If the fielding team fouls, an extra point is given to the team at bat.

The runner is out when:
1. A fly ball is caught.
2. Hit by a ball thrown by the fielder.
3. He does not make a continuous run around the post and back home.
4. He bats out of turn.
5. He does not hit the ball beyond the scratch line.

The game may be timed by innings. Scoring: 2 points for each score made by the runner and 1 point extra if a foul is made by the fielder.

BEAT THE BALL

PLAYING FIELD:	Baseball diamond or playground.
EQUIPMENT:	Volleyball or 8″ rubber inflated playground ball.
NUMBER OF PLAYERS:	2 teams of 9 players each.
FORMATION:	See diagram.

RULES OF THE GAME: One team goes to the field, the other team stays at home base. The batter throws the ball into the field and runs the bases. When the ball is fielded, it is thrown to first base. The ball is thrown from base to base, beginning at first, until it catches the runner. The runner scores a point if he reaches home before the ball. Otherwise he is out. The teams change places after 3 outs; 9 innings is a game. The game may be varied by designating the type of throw that is to be used, e.g., standing sideways and throwing between the legs, or raising one leg and throwing under it. Further variation may include having batter hit the ball into the field.

LONG BALL

PLAYING FIELD:	Baseball field.
EQUIPMENT:	8½″ playground ball or volleyball and 2 bases.
NUMBER OF PLAYERS:	6 to 12 per team.
FORMATION:	See diagram.

RULES OF THE GAME: The team in the field arranges itself as illustrated. The members of the batting team take turns batting the ball from home base into the field with the hand or fist. They may either toss the ball into the air at home plate and bat, or have the ball tossed to them by a pitcher. There is no limit to the number of "strikes," but every "hit" is fair even though it may be only a foul tip. The batter stays up until he gets a hit.

After a hit, the batter must get to long base before the ball or before he is tagged. He may stay there or try to return to home base. Several persons may stay on long base at one time as long as a batter is left at home. When more than 1 are on long base, they may not return home until a hit is made. Each player who gets home successfully scores 1 point. The team at bat continues until 3 outs are made.

A runner is out:

1. When a fielder catches a fly hit by him.
2. When a fielder catches a ball and tags either long base or home base before the runner reaches the base.
3. When an opposing player who has the ball tags him off base.
4. When an opponent hits him with a ball when he is off base.

Variation: Place the base beyond and slightly to the right or left of the pitcher's box.

TEE BALL

PLAYING FIELD: Softball diamond.

EQUIPMENT: Softballs, batting tee, bats, and bases.

NUMBER OF PLAYERS: 18–20.

FORMATION: See diagram.

RULES OF THE GAME: Divide the players into 2 teams. Softball rules are used with the following exceptions:

1. Pitching is eliminated; a batting tee is used. A player fields in the pitcher's regular position.

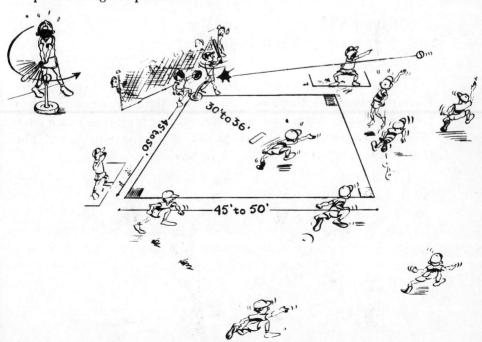

2. A batting tee is placed at home plate.
   a) Batter adjusts tee for his height.
   b) Batter places the ball on the tee, and when ready to hit, calls out, "Ready."
3. Strikes are called if:
   a) Batter misses the ball.
   b) Batter hits tee instead of ball.
   c) Batter hits a foul ball.
4. League games of 7 innings may be played.
5. Players at bat must wait their turn behind the backstop. If a player leaves that position before his turn at bat, 1 out is charged against his team. Players behind the backstop act as retrievers on foul balls and overthrows that go behind the backstop.

Variations:
1. "Work-up" may be played with the tee; use "Work-up" rules.
2. Since "Tee Ball" is excellent batting practice, a player may be given the opportunity to hit the ball 3 times. The batter runs on the third hit and must run the bases and cross home plate before the ball is received by the catcher.

RELAYS

BASE RUNNING RELAY

PLAYING FIELD: Gymnasium, playroom, or playground.

EQUIPMENT: Bases.

NUMBER OF PLAYERS: 20–40.

FORMATION: See diagram.

RULES OF THE GAME: Divide the players into 4 equal teams. Place the players as diagramed. At a given signal, the first player of each team starts running the bases. Each player must touch each base. When he reaches his home base, he touches off the next player. The team first to complete the circuit of the bases wins.

DIAMOND RELAY

PLAYING FIELD:	Playground, gymnasium, or playroom.
EQUIPMENT:	Bases.
NUMBER OF PLAYERS:	12–40.
	Running the bases.
FORMATION:	See diagram.

RULES OF THE GAME: Divide players into 4 equal teams, and place one team at each base. At a given signal, the first player of each team starts to his right and runs around the bases as fast as he can, touching each base as he passes it. On returning to his starting base, he sets off the number two man. The relay continues until all the players have run. The team that completes the run first wins the relay.

GROUNDERS RELAY

PLAYING FIELD: Playground.
EQUIPMENT: Softballs and bats.
NUMBER OF PLAYERS: 20–40.
FORMATION: See diagram.

RULES OF THE GAME: Teams line up as diagramed. The batter tosses the ball up and bats a ground ball to each member of his team, who in turn returns the ball to the catcher. Any ball missed or muffed must be recovered by the player making the play. The batter calls out each round after it has been completed. After each round, players rotate to their left, and the end man takes the catcher's place; the catcher moves into the batter's position. The batter takes his place at the end of the line.

The team having completed the most rounds at the end of the playing period (10 minutes) wins the contest.

FOUR SQUARES BALL*

PLAYING FIELD: Gymnasium, playroom, or playfield.
EQUIPMENT: Volleyball or playground ball.
NUMBER OF PLAYERS: Any number may be in line.
FORMATION: See diagram.
RULES OF THE GAME: Four play at a time.

1. Server "A" serves to any of the other 3 squares by letting the ball bounce and serving with an underhand bat of the open hand or fist.
2. Players always have to bat the ball underhanded with one or both hands.
3. Ball cannot be caught or carried in any way for a return; it must be batted underhanded. The volleying is continuous until a player faults.
4. If a player faults, he goes to the end of the line, and players move up; i.e., "A" faults, "B" moves to "A," "C" to "B," "D" to "C," and a new player to "D."
5. No Chicken Play: this is a movement to remove a player from the game. Every player volleys to the chicken player with a succession of volleys to an inside corner, and then one player makes a quick bat to put the player out. Because of this type of play, it is recommended that players keep in the back half of their squares.

* Contributed by Paul Foster, Alameda, California.

253

4 SQUARES

Faults: The game stops at a fault for rotation.

1. Ball not bounced before it is vollied.
2. Liners.
3. Out-of-bounds ball is fault against person hitting it out-of-bounds.
4. If a ball hits the player, the fault is on the player hit.
5. Illegal hit of ball; e.g., overhand hit.
6. Catching or carrying on a return volley.
7. If a player faults and the next player plays the ball, the fault is then on the one who played the ball.

After "Four Squares" has been organized and the players get the feel of the game, they will begin to establish different variations. Basic rules are necessary to eliminate disputes.

HOME HOPSCOTCH OR SNAIL

PLAYING FIELD: Hardtop, sidewalk, gymnasium, playroom, or hallway.

EQUIPMENT: Chalk and laggers.

NUMBER OF PLAYERS: 2–10.

FORMATION: See diagram.

RULES OF THE GAME: Lag stones to the rest circle. The player closest to the circle starts the game, next will be second, etc. The player must hop on one foot through the squares until he reaches

254

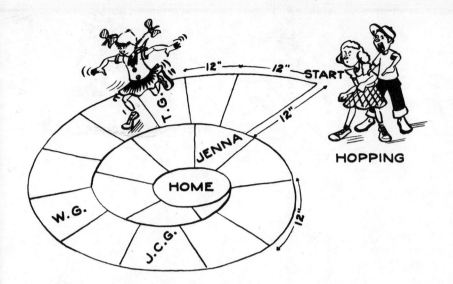

HOPPING

the center circle (Home). The player may stand on both feet when he reaches home in order to rest, he then hops out to the start in the same fashion. Player is out when:

a) He steps on a line.
b) Touches other than the hopping foot to the ground.
c) Takes more than one hop to a square.

After a player has completed his hop to the home and back again, he chooses a square and places his initials in that square. He may use the initialed square for a rest spot, while all other players must hop over it to a square that is not initialed.

The game ends when all squares have been initialed; the winner is the player having the most initialed squares. A player may stand as long as he desires in any space to get his balance.

HOPSCOTCH

PLAYING FIELD:	Hardtop, gymnasium, playroom, hall, or sidewalk.
EQUIPMENT:	Beanbag, wood puck, flat stone, or rubber heel. Hopscotch diagram painted or chalked.
NUMBER OF PLAYERS:	2 or more.
FORMATION:	See diagram.

255

STEPPING ON LINE

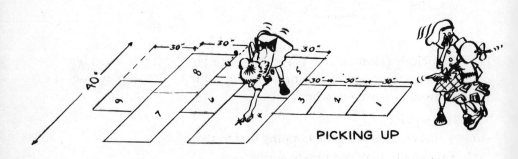

PICKING UP

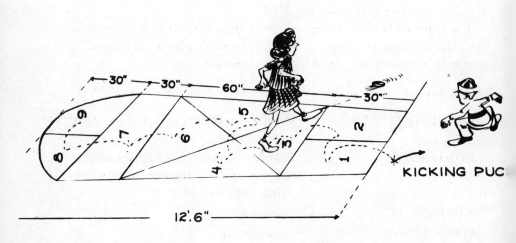

KICKING PUC

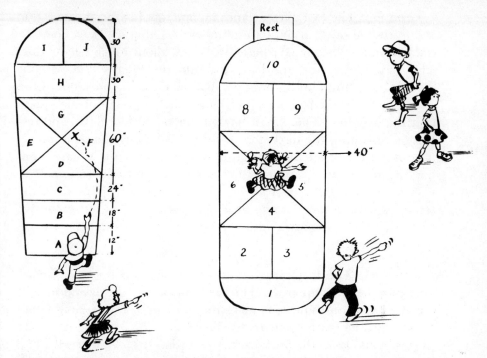

RULES OF THE GAME: There are many methods of arranging the squares in hopscotch courts; they may be painted or chalked on any hard surface. Rules of throwing the puck and hopping from one square or compartment in each court are usually the same, but there are unlimited variations developed by children.

The player throws the puck into the first square, jumps over the square, and lands with one foot in square number 2 and the other in number 3. The player then hops into square 4 on one foot and then lands with one foot in square 5 and one in square 6. The player continues up the court, hopping into each square in sequence, landing on both feet whenever the squares are adjacent (one foot in each square), and on one foot in the single squares. After traveling up the court and back, the player stands in squares 2 and 3, picks up the puck, and hops into the first square and out at the base line. The next turn, the player throws the puck into square number 2, hops into square 1, then into number 3, avoiding the square with the puck, continues up the court and back, picks up his puck, and hops on out of the court. After a player picks up his puck, he may touch his foot to the ground within the area of the square which contained the puck. On each successive turn, the puck is thrown into the next square following the sequence of numbers.

257

Variation: The first player stands on one foot behind the base line and tosses the puck into square number 1. The puck must come to rest within the designated square or space without touching any line. The player hops over the base line into the square, and without touching any line with his hopping foot, he kicks the puck out of the square and over the base line. The player then hops out of the square over the base line. The player may put his raised foot down and rest before beginning the next step in the game. Using the same procedure as in the first square, the player tosses the puck into square number 2. The player hops into the first square and into the second. The player then kicks the puck across the base line and hops from the second square to the first and over the base line. On each successive turn, the puck is thrown into a different square following the sequence of numbers.

Variation: The first player tosses the puck into the first square, hops into the same square, and kicks the puck into the second square. He then hops into square 2, kicks the puck into square 3, and continues until he reaches square 10. The player then changes the hopping foot and kicks the puck back from square 10 to 9, to 8, etc., and back across the base line. If a player completes the above procedure without a mistake, he wins the game. But if the player at any time touches his foot on a boundary line, kicks the puck too far, fails to kick it far enough, or touches the raised foot to the ground, he must leave the court. The next player takes his turn, and when the first player's turn comes again, he must toss the puck into the square in which he fouled during his last turn. If the toss is successful, he continues on from there.

The winner is the player who first makes a complete round of the court.

Fouls that cause a player to lose his turn are:

1. Not tossing the puck into the proper square.
2. Allowing the raised foot to touch the ground.
3. Failing to hop into the right squares in sequence.
4. Touching one of the boundary lines with the hopping foot or the puck.
5. Failing to kick the puck across the base line.
6. Using more than one hop in a square other than the one containing the puck. (Players usually make their own ground rules concerning this situation.)

JACKSTONES, WITH BALL

PLAYING FIELD: Gymnasium, hardtop, classroom, or home (any smooth level surface may be used).

EQUIPMENT: Six to 12 jacks, ¾" diameter and ball, semi-hard, rubber, the size of a golf ball.

NUMBER OF PLAYERS: 1–10.

FORMATION: See diagram.

RULES OF THE GAME: Players take turns competing. The order of playing may be determined in the following ways:

1. Lagging to a line with a jack, a stone, or the ball.
2. Tossing a coin, a stone, or the choice of a number.
3. Tossing jacks: with one toss of the ball, each player in turn attempts to pick up all of the jacks. The player picking up the highest number is the first player.

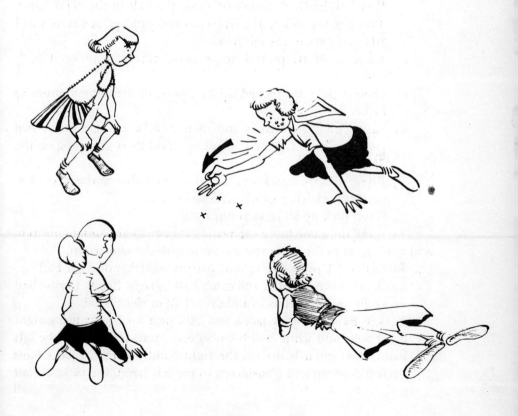

The player who succeeds in being the first to go through all of the following games is the winner:

1. Baby Game	7. Pigs in the Pen.
2. Downs and Ups.	8. Pigs Over the Fence.
3. Eggs in the Basket.	9. Sweeps.
4. Crack the Eggs.	10. Scrubs.
5. Upcast.	11. Double Bounce.
6. Downcast.	12. Bounce, No Bounce.

The following are the official rules adopted by the National Recreation Association.

1. Baby Game: toss the ball up, and while ball bounces once pick up jack or jacks, then catch the ball. This is all done with the right hand. After the ball is caught, jacks are transferred to the other hand.
   a) Ones: scatter all jacks upon the playing surface by a single movement of the right hand. Toss the ball, pick up 1 jack and after ball has bounced once, catch the ball in the right hand. Transfer the jack to the left hand and proceed as before until all 6 jacks are in the left hand.
   b) Twos: jacks are picked up by twos; otherwise proceed as in ones.
   c) Threes: jacks are picked up by threes, in the same manner as before.
   d) Fours: pick up 4 jacks and then 2 jacks, or vice versa, two jacks and then 4 jacks, depending upon their grouping on the playing surface.
   e) Fives: pick up 1 jack and take the remainder on the next play, or, if it is easier, pick up the 5 jacks first.
   f) Sixes: pick up all jacks at one time.
   To make the game more interesting for adults and older children, add more jacks to the game and continue with the same rules.
2. Downs and Ups: all jacks and ball in right hand. Toss ball upward, lay down all jacks and catch ball in right hand. Throw ball up again, pick up all jacks and catch ball in right hand.
3. Eggs in Basket: scatter jacks, toss ball, pick up 1 jack, using right hand only, and while ball bounces once, transfer jacks to the left hand, then catch ball with the right hand. When all jacks have been picked up and transferred to the left hand, the jacks are all

put in the right hand and scattered again. Proceed through twos, threes, fours, fives and sixes.

4. Crack the Eggs: scatter jacks with right hand. Toss ball with right hand, and while ball bounces once, pick up 1 jack with right hand, crack it on the playing surface, and catch ball in right hand, which is still holding the jack. Transfer the jack to the left hand and proceed as before until all jacks have been picked up. Scatter again and proceed by twos. Scatter again and proceed by threes, etc., through sixes.

5. Upcast: scatter jacks with right hand. Toss ball with right, pick up 1 jack with right hand and catch the ball in the right hand after it has bounced once, as in "Baby Game." Toss the ball up again with the right hand, and while it bounces, transfer the jack to the left hand, and catch the ball in the right hand. Continue until all jacks are in the left hand. Scatter again from the right hand, and proceed by twos, then threes, etc., through sixes.

6. Downcast: scatter jacks with right hand. Toss ball with right hand, pick up 1 jack with right hand and catch the ball in the right hand after it has bounced once, as in Baby Game. Bounce the ball downward and transfer the jack to the left hand, then catch the ball with the right hand. (This differs from "Upcast" in that the ball is started on the bounce by turning the palm of the hand toward the ground and then letting go of the ball.) Proceed through sixes.

7. Pigs in the Pen: place left hand on the playing surface, finger tips and wrist touching the surface and forming the pen. Toss the ball upward and while it bounces once, pick up 1 jack with right hand and push it into the pen, then catch the ball in the right hand. Thumb and forefinger are lifted from the playing surface when jack is pushed in, but any jack or jacks left outside the thumb constitute a "miss." Scatter again with the right hand and proceed as before, putting jacks into the pen by twos, then by threes, etc., through sixes.

8. Pigs Over the Fence: place left hand at right angles to the playing area, little finger resting on the playing surface; this forms the wall or fence. Scatter the jacks, toss the ball upward with the right hand, and pick up 1 jack with the right hand. While the ball bounces once, place the jack on the far side of the left hand, "over the fence." When all 6 jacks are picked up, re-scatter with the

right hand and proceed by twos, then threes, etc., through sixes.

9. Sweeps: scatter jacks, toss ball and while ball bounces once, place fingers on 1 jack, and without lifting it from the playing surface, sweep it across the surface with the right hand until it is close to the body. Then pick it up and catch the ball with the same hand. Sweep all jacks singly, then re-scatter and proceed sweeping by twos, then by threes, etc., through sixes.

10. Scrubs: scatter jacks, toss ball, pick up 1 jack and scrub it across the playing surface with a backward and forward movement. Keep jack in right hand and after ball has bounced once, catch the ball in the same hand. Transfer jack to the left hand and proceed until all 6 jacks have been "scrubbed." Re-scatter and scrub by twos, and then threes, etc., through sixes.

11. Double Bounce: this is played the same as the "Baby Game," but ball must bounce twice before it is caught. Play through sixes.

12. Bounce, No Bounce: scatter jacks with right hand. Toss ball upward, pick up 1 jack while ball bounces once, and catch the ball in the right hand. With jack still in right hand, toss the ball upward with the right hand, transfer the jack to the left hand, and catch the ball in the right hand without allowing it to bounce. Continue until all jacks have been transferred to the left hand, then re-scatter and proceed by twos, threes, etc.

Fouls or Misses:
1. Using wrong hand to catch the ball.
2. Failure to pick up the proper number of jacks.
3. Clothesburn: allowing the ball or jacks to touch the body or clothing while catching it.
4. Two hands: catching the ball with both hands.
5. Drop jack and drop ball: failure to hold the ball or jacks until movement is completed.
6. Touching any other jack while attempting to pick up a jack or group of jacks.
7. Double grab: trying twice for the same jack or group of jacks.
8. Double bounce in any game except double bounce.
9. Changing sitting or standing position after jacks have been scattered; plays must be made from original position.
10. Failure to begin a turn with the proper stunt.
11. Failure to comply with the instructions for all games after the "Baby Game." For instance, allowing only one bounce in the Double Bounce Game.

LOOP TENNIS

PLAYING FIELD: Small area. (See diagram.)

EQUIPMENT: One pole made of 2 inch pipe, 10 feet high, set in 2 feet of concrete; one Voit dog ball with a 2″ leather thong threaded through it, and a disk 1″ in diameter placed on the underside of the ball with a knot tied up tight against the disk; a piece of heavy twine tied to the leather thong and attached to the top of the pole, so that the ball is about 3 feet from the ground; two loops, 4 feet from the poll and opposite each other; and two paddles.

NUMBER OF PLAYERS: 2.

FORMATION: See diagram.

RULES OF THE GAME: One player starts the game by hitting the ball in either direction. His opponent must try to hit the ball so the ball will go into either of the loops. If he misses the loop, the other player strikes the ball back trying to get the ball through a loop. This play continues until a loop is scored.

Each loop scored counts 1 point. The player who scores, serves. Game is 15 points. A point cannot be scored on the serve.

ROLY POLY

PLAYING FIELD: Playground, playroom, or hall.

EQUIPMENT: Tennis ball, rubber ball, sponge ball, or golf ball.

NUMBER OF PLAYERS: 2–6. Girls.

FORMATION: See diagram.

RULES OF THE GAME: Playing area may be drawn with chalk or painted on hardtop. The first player rolls the ball from the rolling line to the first square, runs after it, and picks it up inside the first square. If the player succeeds in stopping the ball within the first square, she bounces it on the ground there and catches it in both hands on the rebound. She then steps into the second square and bounces the ball there as she did in the first square. The player steps

263

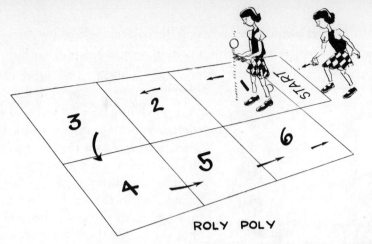

ROLY POLY

into each square in sequence, bouncing the ball once in each square.
While traveling from one square to the next, she must not step on
any boundary line or let the ball touch any line. The first time
through the squares is called "Onesy." If the player completes her
"Onesies" by bouncing the ball successfully in squares one to six, she
goes to the rolling line and starts her "Twosies."

In the "Twosies," the player rolls the ball to the second square,
stops it and picks it up after stepping in square one and then two. The
player throws the ball to the ground and bats the rebound with the
palm of her hand, catching the ball in both hands on the second rebound. She then steps in each of the remaining squares, bouncing the
ball twice in each square. If a player is successful in completing the 6
squares, she goes to the rolling line to do her "Threesy," which is
done in the same manner except that the ball is rolled to the third
square, where she must recover the ball by traveling through number
one and two squares before it rolls out of square three. The ball is
bounced 3 times and recovered in both hands on the last bounce, and
then the player proceeds to the remaining squares, bouncing 3 times
in each square.

"Foursy," "Fivesy," and "Sixsy" are done in the same manner. At
the conclusion of the "Sixsy," a player must "Prove." This is done by
bouncing the ball once in square one, twice in square two, three times
in square three etc.

To make the game more difficult, many other stunts may be added
after a player has successfully completed the "Onesy" through "Sixsy"
and his "Proves:"

1. Swing the right leg over the ball as it bounces.
2. Swing the left leg over the ball as it bounces.

3. Clap the hands once and catch the ball on the first bounce.
4. Clap the hands twice and catch the ball on the first bounce.
5. Clap the hands once or twice on every bounce.
6. Bounce the ball with the right and then the left hand.
7. Bounce the ball, make a complete body turn, and then catch the ball.
8. Bounce the ball and raise the right leg, bounce the ball and raise the left leg, and then catch the ball with both hands.
9. Bounce the ball, hit it up into the air with the back of the hand, let it bounce again, and catch the ball with both hands.
10. Bounce the ball, jump into the air making a complete body turn, and catch the ball in both hands.
11. Stamp each foot once, clap hands, and then catch the ball in both hands.
12. Bounce the ball once and catch it with fists clenched, thumbs up.
13. Bounce the ball in each of the corners of the square.
14. Swing the right leg over the ball and clap the hands as it bounces.
15. Swing the left leg over the ball and clap the hands as it bounces.

At the conclusion of each stunt, "Proves" are to be done before starting the next stunt.

Suggestion: As players progress in ability, it is not always necessary to catch the ball before bouncing it in each square. It even makes an interesting ground rule for the game not to allow catching the ball between squares.

TETHER BALL

PLAYING FIELD: Playground, gymnasium, or playroom.

EQUIPMENT: Tether ball, circle, wooden paddles, and pole.

NUMBER OF PLAYERS: 2.

FORMATION: See diagram.

RULES OF THE GAME: Players stand on opposite sides of the circle; they may not step into the circle. The object of the game is to strike the ball in such a way as to cause the cord to wrap around the pole above the 6′ mark and to continue until the cord is completely wrapped around the pole. The server stands on the service spot and hits the ball with the paddle.

Fouls:

1. Hitting the ball with any part of the body other than the paddle.
2. Allowing the cord to wrap around arm or hand.
3. Stepping over the foul line.
4. Touching pole with the paddle or any part of the body.
5. Stepping into the 6′ penalty area.

TETHER BALL

PLAYING ZONE

PLAYING ZONE

20′ DIAMETER

NEUTRAL ZONE

TETHER POST VOLLEYBALL

HALTER SNAP

Penalty: in case of a foul, play is stopped and the opponent receives a free hit. The cord cannot be unwound more than one half turn before the free hit or serve is taken.

Scoring: a player must continue to hit the ball until the cord is wound around the pole in such a manner that the ball rests against the pole above the 6′ mark. The point is awarded to the player in whose direction it is wound regardless of which player caused the winding. After a score, the loser serves; after a game, the loser drops out, and the winner continues until eliminated.

GOAL GAMES

ANIMAL CHASE

PLAYING FIELD:	Playfield 50' x 100', gymnasium, or playroom.
EQUIPMENT:	None.
NUMBER OF PLAYERS:	Any number, divided into groups.
FORMATION:	See diagram.

ANIMAL CHASE

RULES OF THE GAME: One player is chosen as the Hunter. Each group chooses the name of an animal and tells the leader. The leader tells the Hunter all of the animals he may hunt; the latter calls out the name of the animal he is hunting. The animal group called must run for the opposite side of the playing area, through the forest.

Those who are caught off base by the Hunter become Hunters, and try to catch the other animals as they are hunted.

Variation: In place of animals other names may be used such as flowers, birds, fish, or holidays.

ATTACK THE GOAL

PLAYING FIELD:	Gymnasium, playroom, or playfield.
EQUIPMENT:	8″ rubber playground ball or volley-ball.
NUMBER OF PLAYERS:	20–40.
FORMATION:	See diagram.

40′ to 70′

RULES OF THE GAME: Divide into 2 equal teams. Each team of 10 players is given a ball. At a given signal, each team attempts to throw the ball so that it crosses the other team's goal line. Appoint 4 or 5 goal guards to start the game. After a score is made, teams rotate to their right, one forward filling in the vacated guard position. Team members may move about their half of the field but must not enter the opponents' half at any time.

BLACK AND WHITE

PLAYING FIELD:	Gymnasium, playroom, or playfield.
EQUIPMENT:	3″ wood cube painted three sides white, opposite sides black.
NUMBER OF PLAYERS:	10–30.
FORMATION:	See diagram.

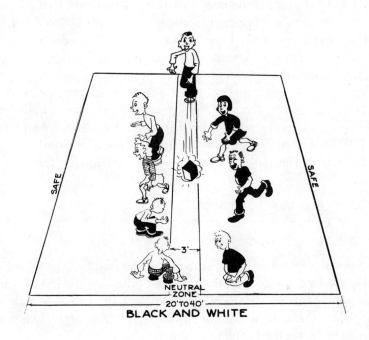

BLACK AND WHITE

RULES OF THE GAME: Divide the group into 2 equal teams. One of the players, the leader, rolls the cube into the neutral zone. If the white side is up, the Whites run for their goal and the Blacks are the taggers. All who are tagged join the Black team; one player may tag as many as possible. When the play period ends, the team with the greatest number of players wins.

Variation: The teams may sit Indian fashion or kneel when the cube is being rolled.

BOUNCE BALL

PLAYING FIELD: Tennis court, gymnasium, or play-room.

EQUIPMENT: Net 2'–3' high, 6" rubber playground ball or tennis ball.

NUMBER OF PLAYERS: 10–30.

FORMATION: See diagram.

RULES OF THE GAME: A player serves the ball by bouncing it once, then striking or batting it with the palm of the hand, so that it will go over into his opponents' court as in tennis. Should the ball fail to go over, the server may have a second try. Server continues to serve as long as his team makes successive points. When a team fails to make a point, the opponents serve.

The ball goes over the net from a service and must land in the court area to count. On returning the ball, the player must let the ball hit the ground, then may dribble the ball from one player to another before driving it across the net with the open hand.

The loss of the ball or a point is the penalty for the following faults:

1. Ball goes out of bounds.
2. Ball bounces twice before being touched by another player.
3. Ball hits the net and bounces back into court or goes dead.

A fault made by the server's side gives the ball to the opponents; a fault made by the receiving side counts a point for the server's side.

Scoring: As in volleyball, 15 points make the game. A team must be 2 points ahead to win game. Teams change courts when a game is completed, and the losing team serves.

BOUNCE BALL

270

CALL THE NUMBER

PLAYING FIELD: Gymnasium, playfield, or playroom.

EQUIPMENT: 8" rubber playground ball.

NUMBER OF PLAYERS: 20–40.

FORMATION: See diagram.

RULES OF THE GAME: Divide the players into 2 equal teams and give each player a number. The highest number should correspond with the total number of players on a team. The leader gives "A" team a ball. The player with the ball calls out a number. The "B" team player with the called number steps out from his line one step, and the "A" player attempts to hit him below the shoulders with the ball. "B" cannot move his feet, but can dodge by bending his knees. If "A" makes a hit, his team scores a point, and the next player on "A" has a chance to call a number.

If "A" misses, "B" takes over and calls a number. A scorekeeper may score the hits, and at the end of the game the team scoring the most hits wins the game.

CAPTURE THE FLAG

PLAYING FIELD: Playground. Vary the area with the age group and the number participating.

EQUIPMENT: One white flag.

NUMBER OF PLAYERS: Any number divided into 2 equal teams.

FORMATION: See diagram.

271

CAPTURE THE FLAG

RULES OF THE GAME:

1. At the beginning of the game, each team places its flag in its own playing area and a guard may be placed near the flag to protect it.

2. Two prisons are formed, one for each team. The prisons should be located about 20 yards from the boundary line. Place one guard to guard the prison, more if the group is large. The guard must stand about 15′–20′ away from the prison.

3. Players from both teams venture into the enemy's territory to find the flag; the object of the game is to capture the enemy's flag and bring it back safely across the boundary line. Players may be tagged while in enemy territory; if tagged they are put into the enemy prison. A teammate may free a prisoner by touching the prisoner's hand while the prisoner has at least one foot on prison. If the teammate succeeds in evading the guard and touching the prisoner's hand, the prisoner and his teammate are allowed to return to their own territory free from being tagged. A rescuer may free only one prisoner at a time.

If the flag is captured, it must be carried over the boundary line. If the raiders are caught before they get back across the boundary, they are put into prison, and the flag is replaced in the same spot from which it was taken. Strategy to decoy players away from the flag should be used to make it more difficult for the opposing team to know just where the flag is located.

At the end of the play period, if neither team has captured the enemy's flag, the game is won by the team which has the most prisoners in its prison. One team should wear a marker such as head band, arm band, or a piece of cloth tucked into the belt.

CROWS AND CRANES

PLAYING FIELD: Gymnasium, playroom, or playfield (30′ x 80′).

EQUIPMENT: None.

NUMBER OF PLAYERS: 10–40.

FORMATION: See diagram.

RULES OF THE GAME: Adjust the distance of the goals to fit the age group. Divide the players into 2 equal teams, one to be known as Cranes and the other as Crows. A leader stands in the middle and gives commands. He may have them march to the center, then give some calisthenics. While they are marching or doing the calisthenics, the leader may say "Crows" or "Cranes." If "Crows" is called, the Crows must dash back to their goal before being tagged; if "Cranes" is called, the Cranes must dash back. All tagged players join the opposite team.

To add to the surprise and fun of the game, the leader may prolong the first part of the word, i.e., crrrows or crrrranes, or he may substitute words such as crrrracker or crrrayfish.

DARE BASE

PLAYING FIELD: Small field or gymnasium; mark a goal line at each end of play area and draw a long line or dare base halfway between them.

EQUIPMENT: None.

NUMBER OF PLAYERS: Any number.

FORMATION: See diagram.

273

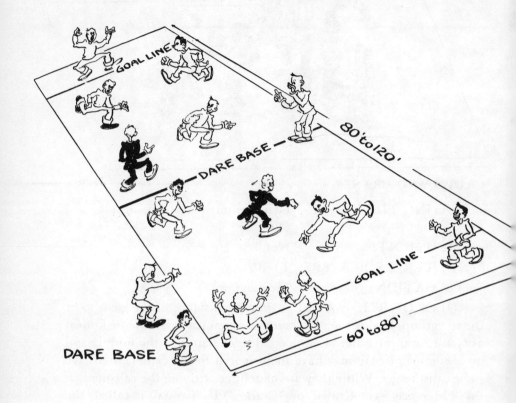

RULES OF THE GAME: Two players are chosen to be catchers; they take positions at opposite ends of the middle line, or Dare Base. Divide the remaining players into 2 groups and place them behind the 2 goal lines. After the game has started, they cross constantly from one goal to another, and the catchers try to tag them. They are safe only when on Dare Base or behind their goal lines. They cannot run back to the goal line from which they came to Dare Base, but must go on to the other goal. Those who are caught are eliminated from the game. The last player caught becomes the catcher for the new game, and may choose his assistant.

← 10' →   50'TO60'   ←— 10' →

END BALL

PLAYING FIELD: Gymnasium, playroom, or playground.

EQUIPMENT: A 6″, 8″, or 10″ rubber playground
ball.

NUMBER OF PLAYERS: 5–15 on a team.

FORMATION: See diagram.

RULES OF THE GAME: Object of the game: the fielders try to
throw the ball to one of their own Endmen. The opponents try to
secure the ball or keep the Endmen from catching it. If an opponent
secures the ball, he attempts to throw it to his own Endmen.

The ball is put into play at the center of the floor by tossing it up
between 2 opposing players. Players rotate to the right after each
score. On the rotation, the ball remains at the end where caught. End
player puts the ball into play after the rotation of players.

Playing time: two half-time periods previously agreed upon.
Change goals at the beginning of the second half.

Scoring: one point is scored when an Endman catches a fly ball in
his end zone.

Fouls: moving out of bounds, dribbling the ball, carrying the ball,
or holding the ball over 3 seconds.

Penalties: the ball is given to the nearest opposing fielder, and play
continues. In case of a double foul, use a center jump.

Out of bounds: fielder nearest the ball retrieves it and throws it to
one of his fellow fielders, and the game continues.

Variation: Corner end-zones as diagramed.

VARIATION OF END BALL

FISH NET

PLAYING FIELD: Gymnasium, playfield, or playroom (40′ x 80′).

EQUIPMENT: None.

NUMBER OF PLAYERS: 10–40.

FORMATION: See diagram.

RULES OF THE GAME: Divide players into 2 equal teams. One team join hands to form the net; they are the Fishermen. The other team are the Fish. On a signal, the Fish run for the opposite goal. The Fishermen try to capture as many Fish as possible by encircling them with the Net. The Net may not drop hands while encircling the Fish, and the Fish may not break or force their way out of the Net. All Fish caught join the Fishermen.

On the next signal, the Fishermen and the Fish exchange places, and the game continues. The team with the most players at the end of the play period wins the game. Sides may exchange every 5 minutes, or when all are caught.

GOAL LINE

GOAL LINE

40' to 80'

FOUR SQUARE DODGE BALL

PLAYING FIELD: Gymnasium, playroom, or playfield.

EQUIPMENT: Four 8″ or 10″ rubber playground balls.

NUMBER OF PLAYERS: 30–60.

FORMATION: See diagram.

RULES OF THE GAME: Divide the group into 4 equal teams, and place each team in a square with a ball. On a given signal, players try to hit someone in another square. When a player is hit, he is eliminated, and must step out of the square. Players may not enter another square to recover a ball, but they may retrieve a ball that has been thrown into or over their square and goes out of bounds.

Players must be hit below the shoulders, and any player hitting an opponent above the shoulders is eliminated. The game may be played as a time game, or until everyone is eliminated from 3 of the squares.

Variation: A hit player goes to the square of the player who hit him.

GUARD BALL

PLAYING FIELD: Gymnasium, playroom, or playfield (40'–60' or 40'–70').

EQUIPMENT: Basketballs, volleyballs, or 10"–12" rubber playground balls; 1 ball for every 10 players.

NUMBER OF PLAYERS: 30–60.

FORMATION: See diagram.

RULES OF THE GAME: Divide the group into 2 teams, and place half of each team on a goal line. Players should stand about 6' apart. The goal line players are the forward; they can not take more than 1 step in any direction to catch the ball. The other half of the team becomes guards, who must be at least 6' in front of their opponents' forwards. They cannot take more than 1 step in any direction to prevent the forward from catching the ball. The guards of both teams try to get the ball to their forwards; they also recover the ball.

Scoring: 1 point for every ball passed successfully to the forward.

Fouls: guard or forward going out of his zone.

Penalty: out of the game for 1 minute.

Time: 5–6 minute quarters; players change positions at the end of each quarter: forwards become guards and guards forwards.

HIT THE FLOOR

PLAYING FIELD: Gymnasium, playroom, or playground.

EQUIPMENT: 8" or 10" rubber playground balls.

NUMBER OF PLAYERS: 10–30.

FORMATION: See diagram.

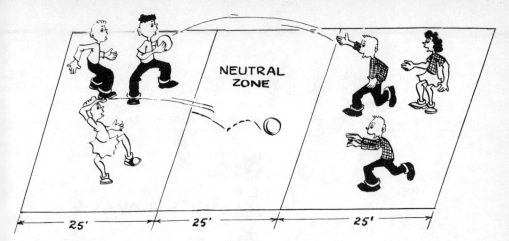

NEUTRAL
ZONE

|← 25' →|← 25' →|← 25' →|

RULES OF THE GAME: Divide the players into 2 equal teams. Place one team in each end court and give each a ball. At a given signal, the balls are thrown across the neutral zone into the opponents' court. The players on the opposing team must catch the ball and return it to their opponents' court. Thus the ball is thrown back and forth over the neutral zone.

Scoring: a scorekeeper should be appointed.

1. A team allowing the ball to touch the floor in their zone gives 1 point to their opponents.
2. A ball thrown out of bounds or into the neutral zone gives 1 point to the opponents of the thrower.
3. A game is 25 points.

Reverse courts after each game.

KEEP AWAY

PLAYING FIELD: Gymnasium, playroom, or playfield.
EQUIPMENT: 6″ rubber playground ball, basketball, football, softball, or beanbag.
NUMBER OF PLAYERS: 10–30.
FORMATION: See diagram.

RULES OF THE GAME: Players divide into equal teams. Teams may be differentiated by having the players of one team wearing a handkerchief on their arms. One player is given the ball, and he attempts to pass it to another player on his team without his opponents' getting it. Players may not interfere with the throwing of the ball, but may intercept any pass. Any player may go after a ball in

KEEP AWAY

flight or a free ball, but must not push or trip. A player fouling must leave the game for 1 minute. The holder of the ball cannot run with the ball or have it in his possession over 10 seconds. The referee makes the count aloud, and if the ball is not thrown within the 10 second period, the referee awards the ball to the opposite team.

KICK-OFF TAG FOOTBALL

PLAYING FIELD: 50 yd. to 100 yd. area, adjusted to the age group.

EQUIPMENT: Football.

NUMBER OF PLAYERS: 10–30.

FORMATION: See diagram.

RULES OF THE GAME: Choose teams and kick off as in regulation football from the 40 yard line. The receiving team spreads over the field not closer than 10 yards from the ball. The player receiving the ball returns it up the field as far as he can without being touched by an opponent. The defending team can touch the ball carrier only with the hands. When the ball carrier is touched, the ball is dead on that spot. To avoid being tagged, the ball carrier may use a lateral pass to another player on his team, who may continue on down the field. Blocking by the offensive team is not allowed. On the spot where the ball becomes dead, the offensive kicks off to the other team which returns the ball toward its goal.

Scoring: A ball kicked over the goal line counts 1 point.

A ball carried over the goal line counts 2 points.

A ball place-kicked between the goal posts counts 3 points.

The game continues for 4 ten-minute quarters.

PLACE KICK

KICK-OFF
TAG FOOTBALL

LATERAL PASS

NOBBIES

PLAYING FIELD: Playground 90′ to 150′; adjust the length and width of the field to the group participating.

EQUIPMENT: Sticks and nobbies.

NUMBER OF PLAYERS: 4–24.

FORMATION: See diagram.

RULES OF THE GAME: Divide players into equal teams. Give each side a different colored jersey or pin a piece of colored ribbon on their arms. Place Nobbies in the center of the field. The teams' centers stand across from each other, left sides toward their goals, with the Nobbies between them.

The referee starts the game by saying, "Nobbies one, Nobbies two, Nobbies three." Each time the referee says, "Nobbies," the first 2 players lift their sticks above the Nobbies and touch each other's sticks, then return the sticks to the ground. As soon as the referee says, "Nobbies three," and the players have touched each other's sticks, they quickly try to scoop up the Nobbies to their goals. After the Nobbies have been put into play, all players on the field are eligible to scoop up the Nobbies with their sticks and throw or run with them.

Scoring: count 1 point for each time the Nobbies go over the goal line.

Fouls: tripping, shoving with the hand, striking a person with a stick. (Shoulder blocking is legal.)

Penalties: player must remain at the sidelines until the next goal has been made as a penalty for the above fouls.

An opponent may use his stick to knock the Nobbies off another player's stick.

Out of bounds: when the Nobbies pass wholly over the side line, a player of the opposite team to that which played them shall throw them into the field. Out-of-bounds play cannot be thrown over the goal line.

Time played in quarters: 8–10 minutes.

Suggestions: nobbies may be made with two rubber balls fastened with a leather thong. (See diagram.)

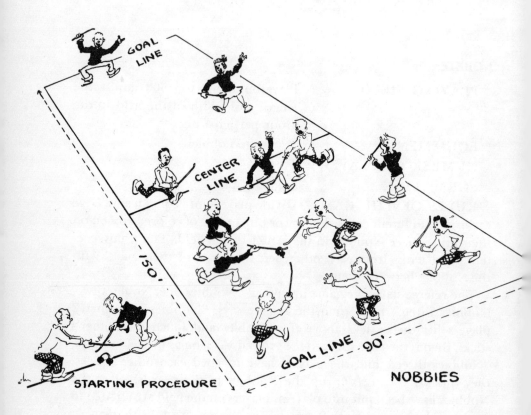

PEE WEE

PLAYING FIELD: Playfield.

EQUIPMENT: Pee Wee (see diagram).

NUMBER OF PLAYERS: 2–30.

FORMATION: See diagram.

RULES OF THE GAME: The regular game (not diagramed) is played in 3 phases, progressing up to the third phase, in which the scoring is made. Usually the game is played as "Work-up," with only one batter, but it may be played with teams. The base is a hole, shaped like the Pee Wee, and just slightly larger. The bat is a piece of broom handle 18″–24″ long, whittled flat at one end.

In the first stage of the game, the batter places the Pee Wee across the front part of the hole. Then, placing the flat part of the bat directly behind the center of the Pee Wee, he flips it into the field (area in front of a line perpendicular to the hole). If the Pee Wee is caught, the batter is out, and the players progress (with "Work-up"). If the Pee Wee is not caught, but is still in motion on the ground, it may be flipped back toward the hole. Next the batter places the bat across the hole, and the fielder who fielded the Pee Wee tries to hit the bat with it from the place where the Pee Wee comes to rest. If the bat is hit, the batter is out, and the players progress. If the Pee Wee fails to touch the bat, the batter goes on to the second phase of the game.

PEE WEE

CUT OFF AN OLD BROOM HANDLE AND TAPER THE ENDS

BAT

USE A PIECE OF PLY-WOOD ETC. ABOUT 3/8″ OR 1/2″ THICK

20 to 24

* BE CAREFUL ABOUT MAKING THE ENDS TOO SHARP

In this phase, he holds the Pee Wee by one end and bats it out into the field. If he fails to hit it, or it is caught, he is out. If not caught but still in motion, it may be flipped toward the hole. Then the batter "fans" the ground directly over the hole with his bat, and the fielder throws the Pee Wee at the hole. The batter may hit once at the Pee Wee as it comes in, to knock it away. If it comes to rest within a bat's length of the hole, the batter is out. If not, he progresses to the third phase, where the scoring occurs.

In the third phase, the batter places the Pee Wee in the hole, the front end extending slightly out of the hole. Then, by striking downward on the front end of the Pee Wee, he flips it into the air, and while it is in the air, strikes at it to hit it into the field. Failing to hit the Pee Wee, or a catch of the Pee Wee by a fielder, puts the batter out. If the Pee Wee is not caught, however, the batter scores points on his hit. The score equals the number of running steps required by any fielder to reach from his base to the place where the Pee Wee comes to rest. Then the batter begins again with the first phase to work up to the scoring stage, or until he is put out.

A simpler version of the game is the one diagramed. The bat is a piece of plywood as pictured, and the base is a circle with the diameter equal to the length of the bat. Only the third phase of the regular game is used. The batter is out if the Pee Wee is caught, or when the fielder throws it at the base and it comes to rest inside the circle. Instead of steps, the score may be the number of bat lengths from the base to the place where the Pee Wee comes to rest; 25 points constitutes a game.

Variation: The game may be played by innings, and the batter may be allowed 3 strikes instead of 1.

Caution: The nature of the equipment provides an element of danger for unskilled players.

PRISONER'S BASE

PLAYING FIELD:	Gymnasium, playroom, or playground.
EQUIPMENT:	None.
NUMBER OF PLAYERS:	6–40. Divided into two equal teams.
FORMATION:	See diagram.

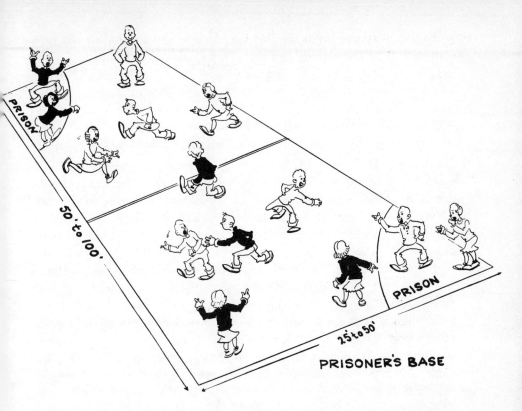

PRISONER'S BASE

RULES OF THE GAME: Increase the playing area according to the number of players and their age level. Players scatter behind the center line in their own half of the playing area. The game starts with a prisoner in each prison. The players try to run through the opponents' territory in order to enter their prison to free a teammate. As players are tagged, they are placed in their opponents' prison. A runner may rest behind the opponents' end line, but once he crosses the end line he must run to his own goal, dodging taggers. Once a player is in prison, he must remain there until he is rescued by one of his teammates. Only one prisoner may be freed at one time by one player. Both players may be tagged after they leave the prison. Once prisoners occupy the prison, the game centers more around freeing prisoners than tagging opponents. Members of each team guard their own prison. Prisoners may not step out of prison.

A team wins when:

1. All opponents have been captured.
2. An untagged player enters the opponent's prison while it is free of prisoners.
3. It possesses the more prisoners at the end of the playing period.

REVENUE RUNNERS

PLAYING FIELD: Gymnasium, playground, or play-room.

EQUIPMENT: None.

NUMBER OF PLAYERS: 10–50.

FORMATIOŃ: See diagram.

RULES OF THE GAME: Two players are chosen to be "It," one in each half of the field. At a given signal, the other players run across the field to the opposite end line. Each "It" tries to tag the players as they run through his half of the territory. Any tagged player becomes "It" and attempts to tag another player. If he tags another player, the tagger stands in the center line holding hands shoulder high with other tagged players. On the signal, the players again leave the end line and run toward the opposite end line. They may run around the players in the center unless they stretch across the field; then they must go under their outstretched arms. If the leader gives a signal, the arms are lowered to hip-level, and the runner must go under the arms or try to break through before he is tagged. The game continues until all have been tagged. The last player tagged wins the game.

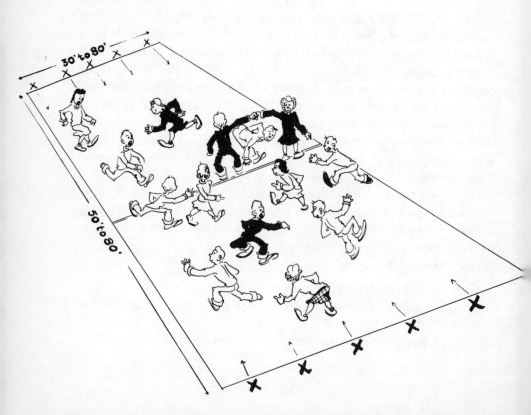

RODEO

PLAYING FIELD:	Gymnasium, playroom, or playing field.
EQUIPMENT:	Two 6″ rubber playground balls.
NUMBER OF PLAYERS:	20–40.
FORMATION:	See diagram.

RULES OF THE GAME: Players divide into equal teams. Team "A," or "Cowboys," number each of their players and place half on each side of the court. Team "B," or "Horses," follow the same procedure. Team "A" starts out with the 2 balls. The players with the balls call out a number, and the "B" team players with the called numbers run across the playing area to the opposite goal, dodging the balls. When "A" team hits 3 Horses, they become the Horses and "B" team becomes the Cowboys.

Score: each time a team player reaches the opposite goal without being hit, he scores a point. If he is hit, an out is scored.

Time: play equal innings; if time runs out before completion of an inning, revert to the score of the last complete inning.

Suggestions: If the ball is in the middle of the court, a player may go out in the court to retrieve the ball. He should throw it to a teammate as quickly as possible. A player may throw at the Horses only from the goal line.

SLAP AND RUN

PLAYING FIELD: Gymnasium, playroom, or playground (30'–40').

EQUIPMENT: None.

NUMBER OF PLAYERS: 10–30.

FORMATION: See diagram.

RULES OF THE GAME: Divide into 2 equal teams. Team "A" sends one of its players over to team "B" whose players have their hands extended. The team "A" player goes down the line, and, after various feints, slaps one of the upturned hands. The one slapped then chases the slapper, who runs for his goal line. If the slapper is tagged, he becomes a member of the chaser's team.

The "B" chaser then walks down the "A" line, slaps one of the outstretched hands, and runs for his line. When play ceases, the team with the most players wins.

Variation: With more than 20 players, have 2 slappers, one "A" and one "B." This will give the game more action.

30' to 40'

STEALING STICKS

PLAYING FIELD: Playground, gymnasium, or play-
                               room.

EQUIPMENT: 12 sticks, 12″ long made from ⅞″
                               doweling.

NUMBER OF PLAYERS: 12–40. Divided into 2 equal groups.

FORMATION: See diagram.

RULES OF THE GAME: Each group appoints a captain, who divides his group into runners and guards to protect the goal. The guards must stay at least 12 feet from their goal, but may go closer if they are attempting to tag an opposing runner. Players stand in their own territory scattered along the center line and facing their opponents' goal.

The object of the game is for the players of a team to run to their opponents' goal and secure the sticks. Runners are allowed to take only 1 stick at a time; they may be caught as soon as they enter the enemy's territory. To avoid being caught, they may return to their own territory.

When a player is caught, he is taken to the prison and must stay there until rescued by some one from his own team. If a runner reaches the enemy prison without being tagged, the prisoner and his rescuer may return hand in hand to their own territory unmolested by the enemy's guards. Runners can rescue but 1 prisoner at a time. The only time a runner may be tagged is while going to the prison or to the goal, or if returning to base without a prisoner or a stick. The game is won by the team which first steals all its opponents' sticks.

Variations: (1) Runner cannot steal sticks if the enemy is holding one of his players as a prisoner, but must release all the prisoners first.

(2) Runners may steal a stick or release a prisoner, but to win the game all the sticks must be stolen from the enemy's goal and all the prisoners must be released.

289

STORM THE CASTLE

PLAYING FIELD:	Gymnasium or playground.
EQUIPMENT:	High horse, parallel bars, or similar objects, all of which should be covered with gym mats when possible.
NUMBER OF PLAYERS:	12–30, divided into 2 equal teams. Boys.
FORMATION:	See diagram.

RULES OF THE GAME: The obstacles should be spread across the gymnasium at the center line. The defending team stands behind the obstacles ready to defend against the attack. The other team stands about 20 feet from the obstacles. At a given signal, the attackers rush forward and try to climb over the obstacles; they must go over the obstacles and touch the floor on the opposite side to score.

The defending team tries to prevent the attackers' getting over the obstacles. To do this, they may stay on the far side to push the attackers back, they may climb to the top of the obstacles to keep the attackers from getting to the top of the obstacles, or they may go over to the enemy's side. Any holding or pushing is permitted, but any excessive roughness should not be allowed.

Each 2 minutes, the attackers become the defenders, and the defenders become attackers. After the teams have had an opportunity to be both defenders and attackers, a 2-minute rest period should be allowed before a change of sides. Score 1 point for each attacker who touches the floor on the opposite side of the obstacles. At the end of the playing period the team having the most points wins the game.

Suggestion: Outdoors, the game can make use of various obstacles.

STUNTS

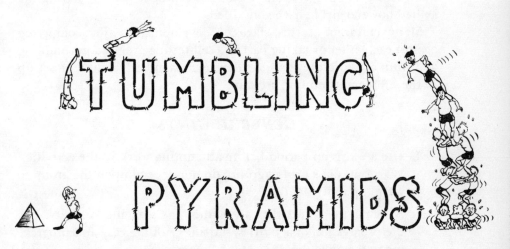

TUMBLING

PYRAMIDS

The physical education program should be organized to fulfill the needs of the modern boy and girl. A limited amount of stunts, tumbling pyramids, and low bar activities has been accepted in the elementary school to help develop coordination, agility, balance, poise, flexibility, timing, and general body control.

Because of the nature of the various activities in this manipulation of the body, boys and girls are able to gain many desirable results and much satisfaction in accomplishment, along with the development of character traits of leadership, courage, and fellowship. When teaching these activities, it is necessary to consider the individual body build and the individual's ability to use his body, for some boys and girls are limited in their capacity because of their physical structure: some are overweight, or have short arms or poor coordination. Therefore, it is necessary to diversify the activities of the program widely enough to give all in a large group of boys and girls the opportunity to realize the feeling of success. It is not necessary for all the boys and girls to become highly proficient in all the individual skills taught, or even to participate in all of them.

The stunts, tumbling, pyramids, and low bar activities in the following pages have been adjusted to fit the different age groups and ability levels by making the activities progressive. Teaching is thus

291

easier, and the children can better gain a reasonable amount of success. When organizing the class, you will recognize differences in ability. Divide the class into ability groups and adapt the lesson to the unskilled and the skilled participants. Through this method you will find the unskilled become less conscious of their lack of ability. Also, many times, the progression of the class can be helped by having the skilled boy and girl help the unskilled.

Many children at this stage of development enjoy competing against each other or taking part in a self-testing program in tumbling and stunt activities; tests and achievement standards should be set up in the stunt and tumbling program.

GENERAL HINTS

I. Use a warm-up period before attempting work in the activities. Warm the class up as a group; do not depend upon the group to warm up individually.

II. Attempt the stunts that are within the students' capacity. Use the progression of activities, starting with the easy and progressing to the difficult.

III. Present the activities on a mat or the grass, and have ample space.

IV. When a child shows fatigue, have him sit for a while. Eliminate children who are not feeling well or have just returned to school from an illness.

V. When doing a stunt together, have the children let each other know when they are relaxing a hold or grasp.

VI. Consider the safety of the student at all times; emphasize to your students the need for safety measures.
   A. Accidents do not "just happen."
   B. Have the students set up safety standards.
   C. Never interfere with one who is doing a stunt.

VII. The times and distances given in the following tests have not been determined in a valid testing program, but rather are included as an incentive to improved performance. Not only will a child strive to do as well as others, but also will compete against himself to better his own efforts. In some cases it may be necessary to set a higher standard of accomplishment for the more capable performers.

FORWARD ROLL

Position: Players assume a full squat position, hands a few inches above the mat slightly ahead of feet, chin in.

Action: Straighten knees and raise hips, placing body weight upon toes (Diagram B). Push off with the balls of the feet. Ducking the head, start the roll at the back of head and neck (Diagram C). Give a final push with the hands, rolling onto the back, with knees tucked in, body in a ball (Diagram D). Keep the chin tucked in, lean forward, chin on chest. Grasp the shins with the hands.

Follow-through: Roll to standing position.

Variations: Arms folded, holding ankles, holding toes, hands on knees, hand on heels.

Hints: Keep pushing with the hands until the top of the shoulders touch the mat. Beginners should tuck their heads down between the knees. Learn to roll on the back of the neck and shoulders. A crooked roll usually indicates an uneven push-off with both feet, or an uneven distribution of the weight on the hands.

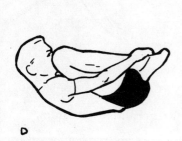

BACKWARD ROLL

(From Standing Position)

Position: Standing position, feet together.

Action: Lean slightly forward as knees are bent. Sit down backward just behind the heels and place the hands on the mat to help break the fall. Reach back with the palms up, ear height. Roll backward, placing hands on the mat. Push hard with hands when weight of body reaches the back of the head and neck. Keep knees well tucked into chest.

Follow-through: Roll over to the feet. Keep hands at the sides.

Hints: Don't throw head backward. Use the standing backward roll after the squat position roll has been mastered.

BACKWARD ROLL

(From Squat Position)

Position: Squat position, lean slightly forward. Wrists are by the ears, hands facing out at the back of the neck, fingers pointing down, thumbs pointing in. Chin on chest.

Action: Reach back with the buttocks and push off hard with the feet. Keep the knees tucked in. Push off hard with the hands while rolling on top of the head. Spread feet.

Follow-through: Come to standing position, feet spread.

Hint: Using the spread-leg ending will help beginners keep their balance.

ASSIST SOMERSAULT

Equipment: Floor mat.

Starting position:
1. Bottom man:
   a) Lies supine on mat.
   b) Knees as diagramed.
   c) Feet spread about 6″ to 8″ and on ground firmly.
2. Top man: Places hand on bottom man's knees.

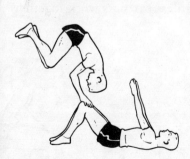 

Action:

    1. Top man uses a double foot take-off to execute a handspring, keeping knees in close and chin tucked in.

    2. Bottom man: places hands on the top man's back under shoulder blades and assists him as he performs the somersault.

Follow-through:

    1. Top man arches back and legs as he comes out of the somersault.

Hints:

    1. Keep knees close to chest on the spin.

    2. Extend legs in landing.

LEG ROCKER

Starting position: pair sit down close together facing each other.

    1. Spread legs and place under armpits of partner.

    2. Wrap arms under partner's knee (as diagramed), and clasp own wrists.

Action: partners work together in rhythm.

    1. Keep momentum going together: one throws his head forward and the other throws his head back to get the rocking motion.

    2. Help with the leg by lifting with the feet under the armpit as head is thrown back.

Hints:

    1. The stunt cannot be mastered unless partners work together.

    2. The head motion is important.

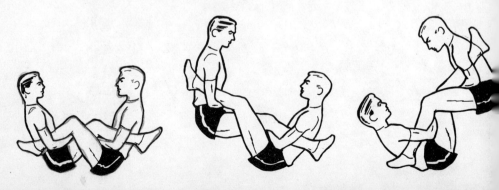

ROCKER

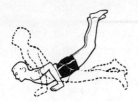

Position: Lying on floor in prone position.

Action: A rocking motion on the stomach, back arched and head up.

HANDSTAND

Position: Place the hands flat on the mat slightly more than shoulder width, fingers spread and pointing forward. Keep the arms straight and look straight ahead. Lean forward so that the head is ahead of the hands. Both feet on the mat, one foot forward and the back leg extended (Diagram A).

Action: Kick the back foot into the air (Diagram B) and follow with the other (Diagram C). Continue the movement of the body and both legs to an upright position. Bring the feet together and arch the body (Diagram E). To prevent a fall backward, flex elbows; to prevent a fall forward, press on finger tips. Point toes.

Follow-through: Duck the head and roll to a standing position.

Hints: Use a wall to improve a sense of balance and help strengthen shoulder and arm muscles. Do not return to mat in an extended position if overbalanced. Tuck the head and forward-roll. Work in pairs; coach each other. Help hold your partner in the correct balance position, and learn to arch the back.

SQUAT HAND BALANCE

Position: (Diagram A.) Squat and place hands on the mat, arms inside of knees and knees resting against the arms just above the elbows. Keep the hips high and fingers pointing forward.

Action: (Diagrams B-C.) Push the body forward with the toes. Keep the arms bent slightly, head up, and press down with the fingers to keep balance.

NECK AND ELBOW BALANCE

Position: Lie outstretched on mat.

Action: Raise the legs up together, keeping the knees straight. Hands on hips, raise up on back side of shoulders and neck, supporting the body by the hands and elbows (Diagram).

ASSIST HEADSTAND

Position: Pair off and assume the same position as in the headstand.

Action: Same as headstand. Partner stands or kneels behind the performer. When the performer pushes up into position, his partner grasps him at the hips, or he may be in standing position and grasp the performer by the ankles.

Use: To help the youngsters get the feel of the three-point balance.

TWO- OR THREE-MAN PYRAMID

Equipment: Mat.

Action: Middle man makes a handstand with the help of two other players.

Position: Two end men clasp hands behind middle man's thighs, thus giving him support. For an end piece on a large pyramid, use the outside man to support the man doing the handstand.

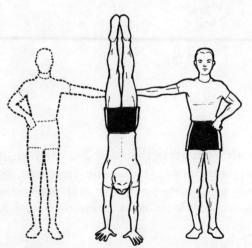

HANDSTAND WITH PARTNER
(Four-Piece Pyramid)

Equipment: Mat.

Action: Two inside men do handstands; outside men help the handstand men to position.

Position: Outside men grasp the ankles of the men in the handstand position, grasping one ankle at a time. In returning to position, let one leg down at a time. Man grasping ankles should let go of one ankle and pivot away from loose leg as it descends to the mat.

THREE- OR FIVE-PIECE PYRAMID

Equipment: Mat.

Action: Two men do a handstand while a man stands between them and supports them with hand on the thighs (Diagram). For the 5 man pyramid, a man stands between the 2 men doing handstands, while 2 men on the outside hold the legs of the men doing the handstands.

BIBLIOGRAPHY

GAMES AND RELAYS:

Bancroft, Jessie H., *Games.*
  New York: The Macmillan Company, 1938.
Hindman, Darwin A., *Handbook of Active Games.*
  Englewood Cliffs, N.J.: Prentice-Hall, Inc., 1951.
Jones, Edwina, E. Morgan, and G. Stevens, *Methods and Materials in Elementary Physical Education.*
  New York: World Book Co., 1950.
Mason, Bernard and Elmer D. Mitchell, *Active Games and Contests.*
  New York: A. S. Barnes and Co., 1935.
O'Keefe, Pattric Ruth and Anita Aldrich, *Education through Physical Activities.*
  St. Louis: C. V. Mosby Co., 1955.
Salt, Benton E., Grace I. Fox, Elsie M. Douthelt, and B. K. Stevens, *Teaching Physical Education in Elementary Schools.*
  New York: A. S. Barnes and Co., 1942.

SOCCER:

Armbruster, D. H., *Basic Skills in Sports for Men and Women.*
  St. Louis: C. V. Mosby Company, 1953.
Blanchard, Vaughn S. and L. B. Collins, *A Modern Physical Education Program.*
  New York: A. S. Barnes and Co., 1946.
De Witt, R. T., *Teaching Individual and Team Sports.*
  Englewood Cliffs, N.J.: Prentice-Hall, Inc., 1953.
Fralick, Samuel, *Soccer.*
  New York: A. S. Barnes and Co., 1945.
Frymir, A. S. and Marjorie Hellas, *Team Sports for Women.*
  New York: A. S. Barnes and Co., 1935.
Meyer, Margaret H. and Marguerite M. Schwartz, *Technique of Team Sports for Women.*
  Philadelphia: W. B. Saunders Co., 1942.
Official National Collegiate Athletic Association *Soccer Guide.*
  Forest Hills, N.Y. Published annually.
Official National Section on Girls' and Women's Sports *Soccer-Speedball Guide.*
  Washington: American Association for Health, Physical Education, and Recreation.
Seaton, Don C., Irene A. Clayton, Howard C. Leibee, and Lloyd Messersmith, *Physical Education Handbook.*
  Englewood Cliffs, N.J.: Prentice-Hall, Inc., 1954.

BASKETBALL:

Armbruster, D. A., *Basic Skills in Sports for Men and Women.*
St. Louis: C. V. Mosby Co., 1953.

Dean, Everett S., *Progressive Basketball.*
Englewood Cliffs, N.J.: Prentice-Hall, Inc., 1950.

De Witt, R. T., *Teaching Individual and Team Sports.*
Englewood Cliffs, N.J.: Prentice-Hall, Inc., 1953.

Hobson, Howard A., *Scientific Basketball.*
Englewood Cliffs, N.J.: Prentice-Hall, Inc., 1949.

Meyer, Margaret H. and Marguerite M. Schwartz, *Technique of Team Sports for Women.*
Philadelphia: W. B. Saunders Co., 1942.

Mussner, Wilhelmine B. and Elizabeth Y. Meyers, *Basketball for Girls.*
New York: A. S. Barnes and Co., revised 1950.

Official National Section for Girls' and Women's Sports *Basketball Guide.*
Washington: American Association for Health, Physical Education, and Recreation.

Seaton, Don C., Irene A. Clayton, Howard C. Leibee, and Lloyd Messersmith, *Physical Education Handbook.*
Englewood Cliffs, N.J.: Prentice-Hall, Inc., 1954.

SOFTBALL:

Armbruster, D. A., *Basic Skills in Sports for Men and Women.*
St. Louis: C. V. Mosby Co., 1953.

De Witt, R. T., *Teaching Individual and Team Sports.*
Englewood Cliffs, N.J.: Prentice-Hall, Inc., 1953.

Fisher, Leo H., *How to Play Winning Softball.*
Englewood Cliffs, N.J.: Prentice-Hall, Inc., 1940.

Geri, Frank, *Illustrated Games, Rhythms, and Stunts for Children: Upper Elementary Grades*
Englewood Cliffs, N.J.: Prentice-Hall, Inc., 1955.

Meyer, Margaret H. and Marguerite M. Schwartz, *Technique of Team Sports For Women.*
Philadelphia: W. B. Saunders Co., 1942.

Mitchell, Viola, *Softball for Girls.*
New York: A. S. Barnes and Co., 1947.

Moren, Arthur T., *Softball.*
New York: A. S. Barnes and Co., 1940.

Official National Section for Girls' and Women's Sports *Softball Guide.*
Washington: American Association for Health, Physical Education, and Recreation.

Official *Softball Guide and Rule Book.*
Newark, N.J.: Amateur Softball Association.

Seaton, Don C., Irene A. Clayton, Howard C. Leibee, and Lloyd Messersmith, *Physical Education Handbook.*
  Englewood Cliffs, N.J.: Prentice-Hall, Inc., 1954.

STUNTS, TUMBLING, PYRAMIDS, AND LOW BAR ACTIVITIES:

Armbruster, D. A., *Basic Skills in Sports for Men and Women.*
  St. Louis: C. V. Mosby Co., 1953.
Cotteral, B. and D. Cotteral, *The Teaching of Stunts and Tumbling.*
  New York: A. S. Barnes and Co., 1936.
De Witt, R. T., *Teaching Individual and Team Sports.*
  Englewood Cliffs, N.J.: Prentice-Hall, Inc., 1953.
La Porte, William R. and A. G. Renner, *Tumbler's Manual.*
  Englewood Cliffs, N.J.: Prentice-Hall, Inc., 1938.